The
Bishop
Comedians
Professor
Brothel
Prison
And
Eels

by

Clifford J. Hearn

Copyright Information

Dedication

To my teacher, the real Mr Oliver, who loved my comedy

Acknowledgement

I would like to acknowledge all the comedians whose talents have made life so enjoyable. I spent my childhood nights listening to them on illicit radios under the bedclothes and then dissipated my youth as those same comedians captivated audiences on TV and in theatres.

My greatest joy was meeting that great comedian Benny Hill whose work still enthrals the world. He did much to inspire this novel. We sat together once on a Mediterranean ferry and he took from his bag a set of English comic papers. His laughter was quiet and contagious. Then he disappeared, unrecognizable, into the crowd.

I never saw him again, except in his work.

Comedians make us laugh when we need to laugh, and make us cry when we need to cry. They give us so much, but we give them so little in return and often they die alone and lonely. They tell us that they merely want to make us laugh at ourselves and cry at our own follies. So a fitting tribute to them is a farce in which we laugh and cry at a set of people who, in some aspects, very closely resemble ourselves.

Clifford J. Hearn
March 2015

Contents

1: Funny Boy

Jerry Seinfeld claims that he was never funny as a child, and so his parents were quite taken aback when he announced his intention to be a professional comedian.

Michael Heron was quite the opposite: he was very funny as a child and earned a reputation as a comedian before he was three years old. As his father, Wally Heron, carried him to the air-raid shelter at the bottom of their London garden in 1940, Michael would be uttering humorous quips that took away much of Wally's agony of getting three kids into the wet, concrete dugout.

"This kid must have been sent by heaven to help us through this damn Nazi blitz," spouted Doris, his wife.

Michael was so funny that neighbours asked if they could share the Heron's shelter.

"Well, I don't rightly know whether we can get more than five of us in here," groaned Doris, but Mrs Cripps from next door was not to be thwarted, "Don't worry Mrs Heron, I'll bring over our camping stove from before the War and we'll soon be cosy. And some more blankets, *and some cocoa, too.*"

Michael was in full voice as they huddled him into the little cot that Wally had made up for him, asking why sausages had the same shape as bombs, and if this was the reason they were called 'bangers' by the British.

There is little doubt that Michael got funnier and funnier as he aged. When he was in the first class at his senior school, he was honing his technique and applying it to his school essays. His English master, Mr Oliver, would ask him to read his work out loud in front of the class, and there would be roars of raucous laughter, led by Mr Oliver himself. On one occasion, the teacher from a neighbouring class came into the room to enquire about the noise. Seeing Mr Oliver at his desk convulsed with laughter, he stopped in his tracks, "Oh, Mr Oliver, I do beg your pardon, I'd no idea you were here."

With a round, smiling face and several chins, Mr Oliver was a somewhat reserved man, and one felt that he was a reluctant teacher and had wanted a completely different career, perhaps as a wealthy accountant. After fighting in North Africa in World War Two, his skin had acquired a light-yellow pallor that lent a reptilian demeanour to his face and hands so that other teachers at the school preferred to keep their distance.

"Come on in, Mr Lauder. Listen to Heron read his essay."

Teaching the boys mathematics was Lauder's speciality and he always walked into a lesson with a cane held up his right sleeve and its end supported in his cupped right hand. Over six-foot tall, he was reputed to be the cousin of Ted Lauder who, a decade earlier, had terrified batsmen on cricket pitches across the world with his fast bowling. The secret of Ted Lauder's speed with the ball was his over-the-shoulder arm-action, causing terror in batsmen when they saw a red sphere aimed at them with comet-like speed from a great height. According to the boys at Winterbourne Secondary School, this arm action was deep in the genes of the Lauder family, and was regularly employed by their mathematics' teacher to great effect with his cane.

Mr Lauder taught boys the simple process of long division, and anyone who couldn't grasp the concept had his fingers whacked. Local employers interviewing school leavers from Winterbourne Secondary always inspected their fingers as the litmus test of numerical competence. Mike Heron's bruised fingers were testament to his failure as a mathematician. Mr Lauder, on seeing Mike standing before a spellbound class, felt an intense anger. Barely containing his rage, he looked at Mr Oliver and then back at Mike, turned on his heel and left in disgust.

Mike was dumbstruck, virtually speechless, and in that moment realised that his chosen career as a comedian was not going to be without the harsh censure of critics. Events were to prove him right, and before our story is finished we shall see Mike sentenced to prison in the name of his beloved comedy.

But, for the moment, his immediate problem was Mr Lauder; after every mathematics class his fingers bled. So much so that he now refused to read his funny essays to the class, in fear that Mr Lauder might burst through the door. Nightmares plagued Mike who awoke screaming every night and it took Doris's motherly arms and hot milk to bring him peace.

Following a concerned letter from Wally, Mr Oliver sought an explanation of the problem, but Mike was tight-lipped and sat defiant with hands in pockets. Finally, the truth surfaced at the end-of-year School Parent-Teacher Day when Mr Oliver talked confidentially with Wally and Doris in the teacher's lounge, with Mike allowed the rare privilege of entering that hallowed space with its carpet and deep chairs.

13

It transpired that Mr Oliver was himself from a theatrical family. During his wartime service in North Africa, he caught jaundice and the army wanted to send him home. Instead, he had opted to join the Army Entertainment Corps where he spent his enlisted time as a Stage Manager, moving with Montgomery's 8th Army to Italy and then joining the Allied Force's advance across Germany.

Stressing to the Heron's the importance of comedy in the lives of soldiers under terrible stress, he smiled with all his copious chins, "Mr and Mrs Heron, comedy does something to us all. If we can just laugh for five minutes it takes away all that tension and fear."

The Herons were amazed by Mr Oliver's directness and felt the sheer humanity of the man.

"I always remember," he continued smiling, "the skit about a soldier standing in a ruined Berlin, surrounded by rubble with every building razed to the ground. Somehow, there was a single water pipe left sticking up two feet from the debris, with a tap on top. The soldier turned on the tap and in his cockney accent sighed, "Just as I thought, no bloody hot water."

Mr Oliver's brother was none other than the famous Joe Oliver, who had created fame for himself as a character actor in the West End of London's theatre district with many movie roles to his credit. Recently, Joe had done occasional comic stand-ups on a radio show called 'Variety Theatre' that aired late on Sunday evenings and was listened to by avid school-boy fans under their bedcovers. For Mike, Joe Oliver was the last piece of joy before the drudgery of Monday morning's school routine.

14

Mr Oliver explained that his brother intended to end his career on the stage. It seems that their mother had died recently and left them money which Joe had suggested be used to start a school for children under sixteen who wanted to become performers. The present plan was to ask the County Council to make some places in such a school available to children who showed special talent and, to cut a long story short, Mr Oliver wanted Mike to go for an audition.

"I think he has a great future," Mr Oliver nodded, his chins folding sideways, "and could become a great comedian. The beginnings of a rare talent are very evident."

We all know that our future can be influenced by our teachers and Mike was forever grateful to Mr Oliver.

Walking home from the School Parent Day, the Herons discussed the prospect of Mike getting a place at this new special school, with Doris concerned that it would be a lot of travelling each day.

"It's going to be clear over the other side of East Walshington which is two buses and a train", she fretted. "That's even if he gets a place."

"Well," voiced Wally with a sense of pride, "it would be a great feather in the lad's cap alright. But I don't know about what happens when he leaves school."

"You're right," worried Doris, "we got to look at his future to be sure. Kid can't divide two by two at the moment."

"Maybe he could get a job in a shop. Perhaps become a butcher. There always seems to be blood on his fingers, anyway."

Doris was shaking her head in dismay. "I want something a lot better for him than that, Wally."

They continued their walk home with it still light and Mike distractedly thinking of a skit in which Mr Oliver's soldier in the ruins of Berlin turns on that tape and hot water gushes out.

Doris was absentmindedly thinking of her sister, Nelly, "Remember how Nelly, got herself in the *family way* working as a chorus girl up in the *West End*. Lucky for her, this damn, wealthy fellow, Bert something, married and looked after her and the kid, what she called 'Denham'."

By the 'West End' she meant London's entertainment district. A 'chorus girl' was a member of the high-kicking dancing troupes whose displays of legs had the reputation of sending amorous men scuttling to stage doors to wait there with floral bouquets, invitations to late dinners, and much more under the bedcovers.

Mike remembered Aunt Nelly visiting one Christmas and her beautiful eyes and body that seemed to invite fun and glamour. Compared to the life of a butcher, the stage seemed to beckon him with all the joy and wonder that we all feel in prepubescence.

"Please, can I at least go for the interview?" he begged, trying to get a word in.

"Good name for a kid, that, Denham," coughed Wally. "Although a mite fancy for people of our class."

Feeling increasingly worried about Mike, Doris snorted "Sounds to me like Nelly and her bloke are putting themselves above us. Already saying the kid's going to University."

These were the post-war years when very few children went to university and, if truth were told, neither Wally nor Doris had any idea what happened in such a place. This was an ignorance engendered by the sleight of hand of Oxford University way back in the year dot when it was the only university in England. Then, horror of horrors, some errant scholars marched off from Oxford and started their own brand-new university at Cambridge.

"We can't bloody have this sort of thing," exclaimed the Oxford fellows. "Before we know where we are the whole length and breadth of England will be full of universities and our privileged life style of doing 'sod all' will be ruined. So they had a little bill passed by the parliament saying 'no more universities'.

Thus it was for many hundreds of years until the Industrial revolution when the country gave royal consent to more universities and before we knew where we were the whole length and breadth of England was full of universities.

"But Doris," laughed Wally trying to placate her, "so much could happen before this Denham kid gets to be university age."

This thought seemed to calm her down and she laughed, "Mind you, my old dad would have loved him to study Shakespeare at university. Dad being so keen on the bard's plays and all that. Remember how he used to dress up and recite them speeches at Christmas."

"Mum and Dad," pleaded Mike, "can I just go for the interview and see what happens. Might be right up my alley. And listen, I can do skits on Shakespeare. I mean I'm up for some of his bawdier bits."

Doris and Wally stopped walking and looked at Mike in amazement.

"I think," whispered Wally after Mike had gone to bed that night, "that *bawdy* means *a bit naughty.*"

"Oh dear me," replied Doris. "Whatever sort of life are we letting the kid into?"

"By the way, Doris, you were mentioning the other day that in her letter Nelly had confessed that she weren't really married."

"I didn't want to say anything in front of Mike, but she just made up that bit about being married so that she appeared to be respectable. But Bertie is sending her money for the kid and promises to see him through university."

"What's she calling herself now? Mrs What?"

"Well, not *his name that's for sure.* Just something she found in the telephone directory, or the place where she slept with this man. Can't remember off the top of my head. Perhaps I don't want to. Anyway, let's get back to our own concerns. Shall we get Mike to this interview? He seems so keen."

Mike Heron was for ever influenced by his mother's starry-eyed respect for Shakespeare and, true to his word, incorporated the bard's love of language into his future comedy act.

2: The Audition

All was set for the second week in June. Wally put on his best suit, and Doris splurged on some material for a new dress which she ran up on her sewing machine. Her face dropped when she saw herself in the mirror on the wardrobe door, and she needed to draw further cash from her Post Office Savings Book to buy a new, all-over corset.

There were thirteen children being auditioned, and the audience consisted of eighteen parents, three grandparents, seven aunties, one uncle, twenty four associated siblings and cousins, the two Oliver brothers, and three freshly-appointed staff of the new school.

The first act was a girl singing excerpts from the Italian Opera *La Bohème,* which brought tears to Doris's eyes. This was followed by a boy juggler who juggled one of his balls into Wally's lap, which was a very welcome event, seeing as Wally had lost one of his own from a sniper's bullet on the Western Front in the First World War. Doris reacted as any woman would, and popped the ball into her bag for, as she murmured to Wally, "A bit of fun later."

The next ten acts were greeted with ever diminishing applause not to mention occasional suppressed jeers. The only memorable events were the ballet dancer's loud "bugger" as she fell off her *entrechat-quatre,* and the conjurer's off-white rabbit making a run for it through an open door to the garden.

Mike stood to do his act with the air of a man who had plodded the boards in every theatre in Britain. Seeing him carry a stool onto the stage, Doris punched

19

Wally in the arm and cried in amazement, "Why that's the stool from the shed what I been hunting for days."

"*Shush*," called the audience, and Doris turned to them, "Don't you *shush* me. That's the stool from our shed what I uses when I'm getting the fruit ready for bottling, and I want it back."

Mike sat comfortably on the stool and announced in his calmest voice, "Today, I wish to talk with you about the question of ownership. It governs all our lives."

The audience started to grimace at one another and mutter, "I thought he was supposed to be funny."

Wally turned to Doris and nodded, "The kid's right you know."

Fairly soon, Mike was relating all human problems to the matter of ownership and gradually making that seem so funny that the audience was immobilised in their seats with suppressed uncontrollable laughter.

Turning to his brother Joe, Mr Oliver nodded his head saying, "Looks like Mike Heron has made the transition from slapstick to satire."

He was right, Mike never again wrote slapstick in his career.

So, at age 15, Mike Heron entered the Theatrical School of Wendsor County and learnt all the tools of the theatre performer, which included voice production and delivery. Mike could be heard in his bedroom at night working through the Shakespearean characters and pretty soon was causing traffic jams in the street outside. So much so that he was soon granted residential student status at the school. It was a mixed gender dormitory building, and the room next-door to Mike was occupied by Skye, who was 17 and taking some of her classes at the Royal School of Performing Arts. She had a part in RSPA's Christmas Concert and told Mike that they were looking for a stand-up comedian.

She was a quiet girl who had grown up near Cayho-on-Thames and had somehow inherited a deep love of comedy. "I think it was from my grandfather who was a butler in London and, as you know, Londoners have one of the most developed senses of humour in the world."

Mike was becoming rather a legend in the Theatrical School and never practiced or prepared his performances, believing that comedy must be spontaneous. In fact, that could be his epitaph. Timing is the essence of his humour: he believed that almost anything can be funny if the timing is right. When TV came back to Britain in the 1950s, after being suspended for the Second World War, Mike was able to watch the famous TV comedians. His favourite was Jack King, who had named himself after Jack Benny. Both those comedians wrote their own material, and both were masters of timing in word and movement. It was almost impossible for them not to be funny. Yet both were very humble, almost solitary men.

3: The Professor

Here we must leave Mike to his theatrical studies and will come back to him later. Now let us introduce Denis Clerk, whose own life and that of his dog 'rustler' would one day be saved by Mike.

Denis Clerk had been in a spot of bother with the police on account of having murdered his wife Sylvia. Well, that is the police claimed that Denis had murdered Sylvia and the facts certainly pointed that way and it was some years before Denis was completely vindicated.

The murder was a surprise to everybody in Telmer St Joseph, where Denis was a respected member of the community. During the day, he drove into Oxenbridge University, just a few miles down the M40 in the West London Suburbs, where he was Head of the Geography Department.

Nobody much in Telmer St Joseph knew what a Geography Department was, but Denis had once spent a great deal of time explaining that it had to do with geospatial relationships; understandably, they never asked again.

For years Denis was a well-liked and long-serving member of the Telmer St Joseph Urban District Council, and became a minor celebrity after he was invited to join the British Commonwealth Committee on Climate Change.

This invitation was quite a shock to the staff at Oxenbridge University since Denis knew nothing about

Climate Change, but the appointment was warmly welcomed by other members of the Committee who felt it would be a good thing for somebody to at least know where all the countries of the world are located. This had followed a very embarrassing situation at the last Climate Subgroup meeting when the representative from Australia had asked why Tuvalu was being flooded, and a member of the committee had replied that they were not responsible for the state of Sydney Super Markets like True Value.

That night, after quite a few drinks, the secretary of the committee, Professor Bill Wolfson, rushed to the membership list of the International Society for Geography, and hazily read that a Dr D. Clerk once had a student who wrote a report on sea level at Tuvalu.

Bill thought it a fair assumption that Dr Clerk of Oxenbridge therefore at least knew the location of this place. So, without further ado, he phoned Denis and, within a minute, Denis was appointed to the Committee for life.

"Glad to have you aboard, Denis," Bill called down the phone and then made a press release that the Committee had appointed the world's expert on Tuvalu to strengthen their work in the West Pacific.

Bill had made a very major mistake in his hasty appointment of Denis, as was pointed out by the Australian Pacific Survey: the work at Tuvalu had been done by a student of Dr Denise Clerk of the University of East Queensland. But the mistake could not be undone, and for the next years the 'Tuvalu problem' continued to be a matter of daily irritation to Bill. His conscience was finally salved in the 1990's when an international committee was deciding on country codes for internet addresses. Bill brought great pressure on them to award Tuvalu the coveted extension 'tv' so Tuvalu's fortune was assured, even as their sand-island home sank ever lower below the waves.

4: The Bishop

Denis's wife Sylvia loved her new fame of being the wife of a renowned expert on climate change. It exactly suited her heritage, since her father was the Anglican Bishop of Gostchester which meant that she was already well-schooled in civilisation's approaching Armageddon.

As a young woman, some ten years earlier, she had a certain allure, which she had used to convince Denis to take her on, first as his assistant, and then his wife. These were not the days when a woman could easily rise in academic or social circles by herself, and Sylvia saw in Denis a man she could manipulate.

Sylvia's father, the Bishop, was himself lacking in intelligence, and so ideally qualified for his post. But, unfortunately, had chosen to marry Magdalena, a woman who suffered from a psychosis that caused her to believe that she was able to fly.

This particular form of mental derangement is not as uncommon as one might believe, and may have its origins deep within our evolutionary past as tree-dwelling primates. In its most lovable form, the psychosis compels small boys to throw bed sheets over their shoulders and jump from upper floor bedroom windows. This is a common cause of entry to hospital emergency rooms. In many cases, limbs do remain unbroken, but the damage from prickly bushes, into which the would-be aviator is forced to make a crash landing, can be very painful. But in adults, the so-called 'Superman' or 'Superwoman' complex is very serious and dangerous. Fortunately, cures, or rather sublimations became available in the last decades of the 20th century in the form of paragliding and, best of all, sky diving. But neither of these marvels of modern living was available to Magdalena.

Although the Bishop tried to keep her on the lowest storey of the Bishop's Palace, almost weekly jumps from high windows caused ever more serious injuries. The Bishop managed to keep much of this from the Church authorities, but it was well known locally, with the Palace grounds becoming a popular picnic spot for those hoping to witness a jump. The local hospital established a permanent, mobile, medical centre on the grounds, and they were successful on several occasions in catching superwoman before she hit the ground. The Bishop was at his wits end after a local scallywag left a broomstick and witch's hat at the front door of the Palace.

Feeling that she needed constantly to try to levitate meant that Magdalena was incapable of being still for more than 30 seconds. Even in bed, she would keep her hands pressed downward on the mattress and yell such phrases as "Ten, nine ... and counting," followed by "we have ignition," and then with arms stretched upwards to the ceiling, "take off." This made any sort of normal sexual fore-play extremely difficult, and added to the Bishop's fundamentalist medieval belief that his wife was possessed of the devil. It meant that his sex life had dwindled to nothing, and he needed a foray into the world of professional courtesans.

Britain has about one hundred thousand prostitutes, and so his search was an easy one, even considering that he needed total discretion and the talents of a woman who would accommodate his highly-developed fantasies.

After one of his twice-monthly visits to the red light district of Liverpool, he was travelling home by train in a happy frame when he hit on a plan.

His Liverpudlian courtesan had been educating him for the last two years on some of the more bizarre and pleasurable varieties of orgasm. Provided the playacting was merely for fun, he conceded that there was no harm in tying a woman down and handcuffing her spread-eagled to the bed. Then had come the added pleasure of pretending that the woman was a witch. We might note that sex shops in Britain do a fairly healthy trade in witch's garb, and keep a good range of sizes in broom handles and hat bands. Interestingly enough, most of the cheaper customs tend to sell out at Halloween, when married couples play their own form of 'trick or treat'.

However, we digress from the particular problem faced by the Bishop, which was that these services were starting to become ever-more expensive and were stretching his stipend from the Church to breaking point.

Every few months, he would go on an economy drive and visit a woman in London who was much cheaper and provided a plain, but quite satisfactory service. It was what he called 'no frills' sex and, if he took advantage of her 'Early Bird Wednesday Special' rate, his monthly budget seemed under control. But these economy drives never lasted more than six weeks or so, after which he was back to his Liverpool lady.

"Where have you been *Jack*?" she would scold him, then add, "I think you'll have to be a bit more severe with me in future, perhaps lick me into shape before you come again."

It was after one such visit to Liverpool that he was sitting on the train deciding that his new plan must be made to work. Substituting his wife for his scouse courtesan would take his sex life from the realm of role-play to reality. As a servant drove him from the railway station to his palace, he felt a pleasurable sensation in his loins. His driver interrupted his fantasy with his well-intentioned remark. "Everything okay with your missionary work down on the Liverpool Docks, your Lordship? I know it's a rough area. Is that blood on your hand? Did you cut yourself?"

Next evening, while the Bishop was being very rough with the woman whom he considered a representative of the devil, his final upward thrust into the depths of her womanhood, sent sperm running for their life where they quite unexpectedly hit an egg which then exponentially multiplied and ultimately created Sylvia.

The mobile medical unit had knocked on the front door of the palace twice in reference to the screams. The Bishop assured them that there were no problems.

Just privately, amongst ourselves, he had surprised even himself with the volume produced by his lungs during his first orgasm, and with added surprise that he could repeat the pleasure twice more; he had made sure his wife was completely gagged.

In view of Magdalena's tendency towards aerial adventures, the gynaecologist who confirmed her pregnancy had signed a certificate confining her to a wheelchair, with an attendant nurse, for the period of her pregnancy.

For those who want to fly, confinement can be unbearable, as evidenced by young nestlings crashing down from nests. So it was with the Bishop's wife. The addicted flyer can be very cunning in the pursuit of their satisfaction, and three weeks before the estimated time of the baby's arrival, the mobile medical team saw the Bishop's wife, arms spread wide, jumping through the sky at them shouting, "Here I come."

The landing on top of their mobile ambulance occurred with such force that Sylvia popped right out into the arms of a waiting doctor whilst her mother bounced skyward severing the umbilical cord and forever curing her insanity. Liverpool's red light district provided a suitable new home for Magdalena where she traded under the name, 'The Mad Submissive Bitch', and made enough money to fly frequently and got to appreciate the joy of having a First-Class airplane seat beneath her.

5: Sylvia

Sylvia had inherited her mother's desire to reach great heights, and took Denis into training as soon as they finished their honeymoon in Bali.

His appointment to the British Commonwealth Committee on Climate Change was a happy and unexpected boost to her plan; the next step would be his promotion to a senior professorship at a more prestigious university, possibly one that had been in existence for more than a year.

Coming to Britain from New Zealand in 1960, Denis had originally taken a PhD at South Helmsford Institute of Technology. His research specialty was the lifecycle of soft corals, and he taught a variety of science courses as a part-time teacher in technical colleges around Britain until he was appointed as a junior tutor in science at Oxenbridge. It was there that he met Sylvia. With a surprising endowment from the Bishopric of Gostchester, Denis set up a Multi-Denominational Chapel at the University and forthwith his promotion was rapid. As soon as he became an assistant lecturer, Sylvia was appointed as a clerical assistant in the Geography Department and allowed to take a part-time degree in any subject. Aeronautical Engineering was attractive as a possible guarantee against developing her mother's flying psychosis. Or, at least, if it proved to be a genetic disorder which she could not avoid, hospital bills could be claimed against the Aeronautics Department.

Sylvia's hit on a plan for Denis's advancement which was based on the simple principle of metaphorically knifing all academic competitors in the back. It is a tried and tested technique and one that she had studied in 'The Art of War by Sun Tzu'. Her techniques were multifarious and became ever-more sophisticated.

In the early days, Sylvia would simply arrive early in a classroom and tell the students that the lecture had been cancelled because the lecturer had been drinking heavily the previous evening. Another ploy was to phone teaching staff and tell them that all lectures had been cancelled for a week, pending investigations of a sex scandal involving Andrew Mathias, who was then head of the department.

Denis rose up through the ranks and became everybody's best friend. Sitting in colleagues' offices was a feature of his day and he would let them pour out all their worries and concerns. A balding man, he seemed to engender trust. His marriage had increased his girth mainly due to daily consummation of some of the best New Zealand red wines. There was something of Charles Dickens's 'Mr Pickwick' about Denis and his jollity was contagious.

Sylvia similarly rose up through the secretarial ranks and soon had charge of all incoming and outgoing mail. With his increase in salary, Denis was able to finance a house called 'The Willows' in Smithers Dell, which is the best residential district of Telmer St Joseph.

Denis named the house 'The Willows' after an old music hall joke that he and Sylvia 'will owe' the bank for the rest of their lives, but he saw the property as an investment on the road to academic fame. 'Smithers Dell' sloped downwards into a dried-up creek known to be the mouth of the River Telmer.

"It does still flow," the estate agent had told Denis. "A very wet summer will see a stream of water draining away. I think there is sort of buried pipe down there. But it's all well below the house. You could make an aquatic feature of it with a few rocks and plants."

So, 'The Willows' became the scene of several dinner parties each week. One special party had included Geoffrey Tate, Head of the Department of Aeronautical Engineering. He took the opportunity to ask Sylvia why she had never attended any lectures or examinations, although registered as a student for the last six years. During dinner, he became so drunk on Sylvia's zabaglione dessert that he tried to put both hands down the front of her deliberately low-cut shirt. The following week she had a letter from the University saying that she had been awarded a pass degree 'in absentia' for her outstanding thesis on Italy's contribution to the theory of flight. The letter added that her thesis had become lost in administrative reorganization and if she had a spare copy please could she pop it into the University Library for their archives. This meant that Sylvia was now a graduate and could be formally promoted to Head of Administration in the Geography Department.

6: Skye

It's time now to see how Mike Heron is getting on with his life, along with his student friend, Skye.

Just as he had promised his parents, Doris and Wally Heron, many of Mike's skits were adapted from the bawdier parts of the works of the great British bard, William Shakespeare. The jokes that Mike created had kept him and Skye laughing through some very difficult times, including the Asian influenza epidemic of the late 1950's. Most of the students at the Theatrical School of Wendsor County contracted the disease and many died. Mike knew that he had fallen victim to the flu but refused to report to the sick bay and be put straight into a bed which lay unchanged since the last student died there. Instead, he stayed in his own room and claimed to have hurt his ankle. The critical moment came one Sunday evening. Turning on the portable radio that his parents had given him last Christmas, he knew he must listen to music all night and not close his eyes.

Closing one's eyes is an admission that one can fight no longer.

With eyes still open next morning, he knew he had survived but was worried about Skype who insisted on going to the sick bay where he sat by her as she coughed and fought for life.

"Skye, many people question how the first virus could have evolved on Earth. What evolutionary advantage is there to a virus in killing animals? Surely it came from space; maybe *Star Wars* have been ongoing for millions of years and the inhabitants of some distant planet beamed the first virus at us."

"I'd say, Mike, they've got a winner with this Asian flu. I never felt so sodding awful in my life."

Like Mike, Skye had that wonderful English humour and total irreverence for all things sacred. "But," she choked, "can't hear any heavenly bells yet. Perhaps the ringers don't work on Wednesday evenings."

"Skye, it's Saturday morning."

"Bloody hell, don't tell me they have Wednesday evenings *and* Saturday mornings off work."

Mike could feel tears and fought hard to hold them back. His face scrunched up and he swallowed as hard as he could, but it was no use.

Pulling her right arm free of the bedclothes, she gently rested it on his knee.

"Mike Heron, I'm going to say goodbye now, *but* before I do, I want you to make me a promise. *Okay?*"

His head was bowed low, as he looked at her hand and then put his own over it.

"Mike, I want you to promise me you'll be famous. And I mean *Bloody Famous*. Okay?"

He croaked back, rather prophetically as it is to turn out in our story, "You mean *h'im-famous*."

"You are so clever with your words, Mike" and then nearly choking, so that the nurse came and held an oxygen cup to her for a full minute, she added, "You're the funniest bugger that I ever met. First time I ever saw you I thought that I would die laughing, and now, the last time I'm seeing you, I *am* bloody *dying laughing*."

He waited as the nurse tried to take Skye's pulse but she was starting to feel really unwell herself and just leaned across and closed Skye's eyes; this was the sixth student to die before her that day.

Early next day, Mike left school and spent two years in the Army. Never once was he funny, but he spent his free time writing down all the sketches that he and Skye had devised.

Also early next day, Skye raised herself off the mortuary slab. Her years of training at the Royal School of Performing Arts had taught her to die well. She returned to her room collected her things and set off to join a company of strolling players and learn the real art of entertainment. In that moment, Skye ceased to exist; the records at the Theatrical School of Wendsor County showed she died of the Asian influenza.

After the Army, Mike applied for a job as a stage-hand at the Windmill Theatre in London's Soho District. The audience were all men who came to see the naked girls on stage. Every half-hour a comedian would appear, and the audience would read their newspapers and jeer. Not many comedians could endure this treatment for more than a few days, but the law demanded that the Windmill was primarily a comedy club, and without the comedians there could be no nude girls. The only rule from the Lord Chamberlain was that the girls were not allowed to move. So the audience was hell set on getting a bit of movement. As one sailor was heard to say as he left the Windmill, "Smashing. Bloody smashing. I likes a bit of tit and that mouse what the fella in the front row dropped on stage did the trick for me."

Mike's job was to hand out wraps to the girls as they left stage. One evening Jimmy Wallis, 'the laugh-a-minute wonder from Rochester' ran off stage crying, "I've been hit in the eye with a used condom. Saw the bloke from the wings jerking off while watching the girls. Bastard. I'm out of this dump forever."

Two seconds later, after a nod from the stage manager, Mike was asking the Wednesday evening audience, "Which one of you put that notice on the condom vending machine in the men's room saying: *this is the damnedest gum, I ever did taste.*"

Instantly he had their attention, and for three months there was a line of men and women waiting to get into the Windmill. The theatre started to run four shows a day and needed to recruit many new girls and other staff. Mike's name was in three-foot-high neon lettering and there is no doubt that this was the genesis of the association of Mike's name with the exhibition of the female body. It was good for trade but slightly unfortunate for Mike because eventually was to come a female backlash.

Two years as a touring stand-up comic took Mike through the working men's clubs of Britain's major cities and then to the USA, where he toured the comedy clubs. After one evening performance in New York, he strolled the theatre district and stood watching a troupe of street clowns.

"Please ladies and gentlemen gather around more closely, else the police will move us on for blocking the pavement. I mean the sidewalk. You sir," and the clown pointed at him, "I must have you up close to me." The crowd laughed and Mike walked forward. That voice so

40

familiar. The hat went round for money, and he pushed in a twenty-dollar bill.

"That's very generous, sir." The same clown smiled with those huge white bulbous lips and eyes that were surrounded with heavy red paint.

"It was a first-class, unforgettable performance."

Their eyes met, and the clown continued, "Praise indeed from a comedian of your standing, sir. You are Mike Heron, I believe."

Mike shivered, and the blood left his face, "Skye? What?"

It's hard to believe your eyes when you suddenly see a long-ago loved one that you thought dead.

"No, sir. Name's Humpy the Clown, sir, and here's my business card in case you're hiring for a TV show or something. Good night, sir." Then, spreading her arms to include the crowd of clowns around her, she said with some finality, "We need to move further down the street."

As Humpy spoke, a short clown cartwheeled between them and Mike read his jersey as 'Tiny Tim'. Mike watched, somewhat dumbfounded, as this Humpy the Clown and her entourage moved on down the street. He wanted to run after them, but somehow his feet remained glued to the sidewalk.

To see a ghost is something that happens to us all sometime in our lives. We meet a person whom we feel we know, and they deny us. Mike walked into a café, ordered cheese cake and coffee and read the card: Mr Humpy. World Famous Clown. Phone 893 748 HUMP.

7: Two for the Price of One

Meanwhile, back at Oxenbridge University, let's check in on Sylvia Clerk, Denis's wife, and see exactly what happened once she had cheated her way into the new post of Head of Administration in the Geography Department.

Her first initiative was to seek out British and European prizes for outstanding postgraduate students and arrange for them to be awarded to the weakest students in Geography without telling their advisors or supervisors. The annoyance and fights which followed led to the resignation of Andrew Mathias, the Head of the Geography Department, following the death of one of his staff, Roy Bolger, who had hit him very hard in the face and then panicked and ran away, mistaking the fifth-floor window for the way out.

Sylvia was the first into Andrew's office after the assault and gave him succour as soon as she had picked up the exit sign and put it back in its proper place. This ploy followed a suggestion by Sylvia's mother, who was now the Madam of one of London's most exclusive brothels called 'Flights of Ecstasy', conveniently situated just a two- minute walk down a very dark alleyway that ultimately connected to the Houses of Parliament.

With Andrew's departure, Denis took over as Head of the Geography Department and he and Sylvia worked on his appointment to many powerful International committees. Sylvia's mother was helpful in this project by printing 'Two for the Price of One' gift vouchers, which found their way into the pockets of all international committee members invited for dinner at The Willows. This was accompanied by Sylvia taking a three-month leave of absence from the University, during which time she worked as a mistress at her mother's brothel. She found this very satisfying in a variety of ways and always worked wearing a mask. If the client produced a 'Two for the Price of One' voucher she doubled the time spent using her tongue and then removed her mask as she walked him arm-in-arm to the discrete side entrance, finally giving him Denis's best regards.

This went well, and Denis was soon offered senior posts in larger and older universities. Accompanying him on an interview in Chelsea to become President of the newly created London School of Technology, Sylvia studied the appointment board. It consisted of four men and one woman, all of whom held senior posts in Education, Government, or Industry. As is usual with interview committees, their prime interest was personal gain rather than the good of the institution.

Sylvia played them at their own game.

After Denis's interview, Sylvia dressed as a waitress at the Committee's smorgasbord and drinks session in the Dorset Room at the Chelsea Tropicana Hotel. Their purpose was to finalise their choice of the best candidate.

The group mingled, and Sylvia managed to get eye to eye with Sir Guy Holmes who whispered, "If you're free later tonight, I'd like to slip inside you. Sorry, I don't have a voucher, but I do have five thousand in cash and ten times that if you'll spend a weekend on my yacht in Cairns."

Sylvia's plan was at risk of backfiring. Her aim had been Denis's promotion by blackmail, but her bluff had been called. In that moment she realised that she could make more money and have more power as a courtesan than by promoting Denis. This confirmed her mother's advice whilst she was working part-time at 'Flights of Fantasy'.

"Besides which, Sylvia," her mother had added, "I'll need somebody to take over here soon. Time for me to retire and spend some money getting all those old, head injuries attended to. Mind you, in recent years my chin has also been injured by being hit by so many *balls*."

Now at the drinks session, Sylvia stared back at Sir Guy Holmes and demanded, "One condition. Appoint Denis to this post."

"Never in a thousand years."

"Why not?"

"He's a crook. A shameless New Zealand upstart."

"I'll tell them about your brothel visits."

"I'll tell them you're a whore. A good one, but still just a whore."

So, she took the five thousand and further agreed to spend the next weekend very lucratively on his yacht presently anchored in the Mediterranean. The lie to Denis was to be that she had also been offered a job at the School of Technology, as Head of Administration, and was invited to visit Cannes École Normale Supérieure, which was to be the model for the London School of Technology, already being referred to as 'LST', "although," cautioned Sir Mark with a lowered, shaking head, "we dearly hope that it's not going to give us as much bloody trouble as LSE."

One of the great problems of obtaining success through malice to others is that, eventually, the victimized will seek revenge. One such was Celia Bolger, the wife of Roy Bolger who had been killed by walking out the office window of the Head of Department, Andrew Mathias, after punching him in the face. Sylvia had been the first onto the scene and Andrew, dazed as he was, reported seeing her take down the exit sign from the window through which Roy had just departed.

The ballistics of falling bodies has a depressing regularity about it and, despite the old adage that a cannon ball never strikes twice in the same place that is exactly what happens. For those doubting my words, I refer to the Royal Navy report of 1810, by Admiral 'Peg-Leg' Peterson and First Sea Lord 'One-Armed' Owens who both got their comeuppance in the same cabin, but in different battles in 1782, on HMS Victory.

But, I digress. Looking downwards through the window of Andrew's office, Sylvia saw Roy's body spread eagled in the car park and realised he had only just missed Denis's reserved parking place. Had she known of the Mortimer-Murphy report, then available in the Oxenbridge University library, she would have insisted that Denis apply for a new parking spot.

Celia Bolger spent the next many months investigating the circumstances of her husband's death. Her research included interviews with all staff in the Geography Department and, given Andrew's incriminating recollections, Celia had spent months tailing Sylvia, which included her days at 'Flights of Fantasy'.

On the day of the interview in Chelsea, Celia had followed Sylvia to Sir Guy Holmes hotel and listened outside his door. It was easy to get the front desk to issue a spare key and, at 1 am next morning, she posted pictures of Sylvia, in a very compromising position, on all the notice boards in the Geography Department; the fifty, one-hundred-pound notes were in evidence on Mark's bedside table.

Denis arrived at work that morning at 6 am and seeing the photos called Sylvia at home in a state of extreme distress but did not disclose the reason. Instead, he suggested that she should take a rest day at home and then come into his office later so that they could go out to dinner. Sylvia was happy to obey and took the opportunity to laze in bed, knowing that she had a busy weekend ahead.

Not all academics are early risers but by 10 am, most Oxenbridge University staff had been forced out of bed by phones ringing with the gossip, and the University was abuzz with advice for Denis.

At 6 pm, Sylvia took a taxi to the University and arrived after ten flights of stairs in Denis's office. He pushed the photographs at her. The alarm on her face could not be easily hidden, but, thinking quickly, she started to explain that it would ensure Denis's appointment at LST. Asking to see her brief case, Denis found, as expected, the five thousand pounds tucked into one of its hidden compartments.

Shaking his head in disbelief, he allowed Sylvia to wrestle back the brief case and hold it under her arm. With Denis's face contorting in pain, Sylvia was filled with guilt, panicked, and rushed towards the door of the office in a state of mental turmoil.

The notice marked 'Exit' was now illuminated following the terrible tragedy of Roy Bolger, but it fired a train of thought in Sylvia's guilty mind.

Stopping abruptly, she smiled, "Nice try Denis, but you're not getting rid of me that easily," as she turned away from the illuminated Exit sign and walked out the window.

Sylvia's mother had told her long ago that jumping out of a high window is a lot of fun.

'The higher the better', and 'oh what joy it is'.

'Like a bird'.

There is a feeling of total freedom as you fly weightless for what seems like eternity, and, unfortunately, may well actually be eternity.

It always seemed to Sylvia's mother that things had worked well for the birds. It was now agreed by scientists that our modern birds evolved from dinosaurs.

The dinosaurs would sit around in the evening realizing that it would be a few tens of millions of years before beer was invented. Some of the younger one's wondered what beer would taste like, but they all seemed to agree on a couple of things: it needed to be cold and best served in bottles. The Sauropods suggested that long-neck bottles would give a greater cushion of air to enhance the pleasure of the aeration. As for smart phones, or more importantly burgers and chips, well they had no idea.

Then along came a huge asteroid and it was all over for them. Later, sitting around in Heaven, they thought to try something different, and decided to evolve into birds.

That was so very clever of them.

Humans had all the same choices but, despite their bigger brains, had not checked the evolution box marked: 'do you want to fly?' That was except for Superman and Robin, of course.

To Sylvia's mother being able to fly was a definite must on her list of personal achievements.

As Sylvia fell from that tenth storey window, she at last began to understand her mother. That in itself was good since most of us go our whole lives without understanding our parents; when you're young, they are just a constant nightmare telling you not to stay out late and then suddenly they're old asking you for a hand-out or wanting to come and live with you.

So for Sylvia it was good, albeit only in the last second of her life. Her mother had been what the medical experts call a 'bouncer'. Sylvia was not. The difference between a bouncer and what the medics call 'a dead weight' is a matter of body fat, muscle tone and balance. Despite the extremely thorough 'seeing to' that she had received from Sir Mark, she was in poor condition before and even worse afterwards. In fact coming home in the taxi she had preferred to be prone on the back seat; now she realised why there are no statues of Ancient Greeks sitting down.

Sylvia hit the ground in the main staff parking area and died instantly. It was exactly the spot where Roy Bolger had breathed his last breath and proved that old 'Peg-Leg' Peterson and 'One-Armed' Owens where exactly right in their supposition that cannon balls, and any object really, released identically tend to fall in the same spot. Sylvia's dying thought was that Denis had not made arrangements for their allocated parking space to be relocated. As she died her shiny metal brief case, bought for her as a present from Denis last Christmas, shot out of her hand and slid fifty feet across the parking area. It bore a label with her home address and was posted on to her that evening by a well-wisher who first put the 5000 pounds in a secure place, which was, conveniently, their wallet.

Denis had screamed.

But no one heard him. Geographers are not ones to work late and being alone in one's office after 4 pm when Denis was still in the building could invite a visit from him that resulted in more teaching assignments. All prospective new staff are inclined to cite a love of teaching on their application forms and many of them do have that love until they see their first examination answers which cause them a sickness which can only be alleviated by a continuous stream of alcohol fed directly to the blood stream.

So the scream just echoed around the empty building, completely unnoticed. It was what we call a panic scream and consisted of both high notes and long deep chords. Such screams tend to change their sound with time due to what scientists all-knowingly call 'dispersion'; they find that a very important pick-up line with girls in low cut dresses at drunken parties. To let you into the secret of this exoteric chit-chat, it basically means that the high and low sounds get separated. So Denis's scream finally crept back into his office but over a one minute interval. First were the high frequency notes, all sprite, lively and cheeky, followed much later by a long low, exhausted hiss which he mistook for an anal escape of wind from his terrified body.

The Geography Department was without a lift. This was a personal achievement of Bill Grossman who claimed that Geography Departments are just a way of recruiting students whose only ability is to pinpoint the nearest pub on a map.

"Bad enough having one of these damn geography caverns," Bill had yelled at the University Building Committee, of which he was chair, "but there is no way they're getting a lift, that is an *elevator* in Americanise. Just tell me, who was the last person to get a Nobel Prize for *geography*?"

"Bill that is unfortunately true," cried Chris Croppers, the Head of Chemistry, who wore, as always, a freshly laundered crisp white lab coat with an ancient hole in the sleeve which he boasted to be an acid spill when a student. His desire to side with Bill Grossman, who was undoubtedly the most powerful academic in the University, came from his secret worry about the lack of new chemistry students. Worst of all, he had nightmares over the rumour that the University was hatching a plan to combine Chemistry with the new, highly popular, 'Agricultural Studies'; he imagined the students coming to class in Wellington Boots armed with shovels.

Bill was in full voice, "Thank you, Chris. Bloody Geography. Okay, tell me one thing that a geographer can do that I can't do myself?"

"Well," lisped Derek Young, the flowery new assistant Registrar, rather meekly, "They are good at folding up maps." He checked that his bowtie was entirely straight and secretly congratulated himself on its shade of purple when worn with his very light blue shirt. "You know, the way you can never get the folds to line up again. So very annoying. Can completely ruin one's day."

Bill was speechless and sat there with mouth open. "Okay." Shaking his head, "Okay. Yes, I suppose so."

Then with a roar, "But *no bloody lift*."

So Denis ran down all those flights of stairs and across the parking area. There she was beside his car. It was just too easy: open the back of the car and haul her in. Just like that. A passing security guard smiled and asked, "How's it going Professor Clerk? Don't you go worrying about those photographs. Word is that they are promotional shots for the Christmas play, 'The Price of Infidelity'. But I got to say this, Professor, they really are very realistic."

"Yes, just a bit of good publicity we got done for the play," replied Denis nonchalantly as he drove away.

Denis's subsequent actions were not well considered. You know those moments in your life when you make an instant decision that will affect you for evermore. In Denis's case he simply made no decision at all, but drove home.

Criminologists have debated Denis's actions, or rather lack of actions, but in his defence, most people agree that had if he driven to the police station the police were very unlikely to have believed his story.

My own view, for what it is worth, is that if somebody comes into your office and jumps out the window, you should do nothing. Just don't get involved. But, on the other hand, in Denis's case, there were all those photographs which seemed to involve him in some sort of dispute.

Denis's father had been a country butcher and had slaughtered sheep and prepared the meat for sale. As a young boy, Denis had helped his dad. When the old man died six years ago, Denis went home to New Zealand for the funeral in a state of extreme nostalgia, typical of New Zealanders who live abroad, which is most of the nation. Denis wanted to ship back to Britain a souvenir and chose, very understandably, a meat saw. Its arrival in Telmer St Joseph caused Silvia to comment, "Why the hell have you shipped that bloody thing here?"

Unanswered questions can often be prophetic. But she would never know that.

What to do with a dead wife? It's a question that in reality faces few men in their lifetimes but, nevertheless, is one dreamed of by most. Being a geographer, there was much in the world that Denis did not understand, and the working of that creature called the human female was one of which he was daily aware. So much so, that he had joked to a colleague at the University Staff Club one Friday evening, after three bottles of 'Kiwi Old Dog Export Special', "*Women*. Who understands them? If I gave you a kit with all the parts, bet you couldn't put one together."

Denis backed his car into his garage and it took one push for the body to roll out onto the concrete floor.

"Might as well put the car on the road tonight so I don't need to be bothered driving around her in the morning," Denis muttered in a rare moment of real planning. "By the way, it looks like I don't have to eat one of her bloody awful healthy breakfasts in the morning." After checking the fridge, he drove to the local supermarket for eggs, New Zealand bacon and, as an afterthought, some New Zealand wines, a case of beer, and a bottle of Jack Daniels.

Very few of us have not woken with a hangover at some stage of our lives and so we all know those waking minutes contain some standard features. Foremost is a resolution to become teetotal or at least not to touch alcohol for a year, well at least a week, well, not to have a drink today. That is until after dinner.

The next feature is, "Am I alone or is there somebody else in bed with me whom I may not recognize?"

Turning his head very carefully from side to side, and squinting his eyes open against the light, revealed no foreign bodies - but also that he was not in bed - but lying fully clothed on something hard made of wooden slats. There was also the worrying lack of shoes and spectacles.

Denis closed his eyes and thought about possible locations for his body. Then he remembered that very bad London party some years ago when he awoke on a railway platform bench that turned out to be Thurso in the far North of Scotland.

Denis listened for ambient sounds then reached out and found smooth hair and a soft tongue on his face. "Wows, Sylv, seems like we made a night of it. Where are we?"

Then came the third feature of waking after a night of excess alcohol: the memory of something terrible. Something happened last night. What was it?

Opening his eyes fully, he remembered everything. Well, almost everything. There was an immediate discomfort to his back. Trying to move he realised that he was on the bench in his own garage. Worst still next to him lay 'Rustler', his rather diminutive Yorkshire terrier who had forsaken his dog basket for the greater intimacy of Denis's warm body.

Rustler had often been told stories by neighbour dogs that many of them were allowed to sleep with their owners on their beds whilst he was barred from even entering the house and had to be content with a cheap uncomfortable basket. Most nights he simply chased the one dog pillow round and round the basket and usually ended up on the hard concrete floor. So last night had been a dream come true and he was able to cuddle with Denis.

Then Denis realised that below him on the concrete floor lay a dead body.

Other people dying are really a confounded nuisance, and there should be special bins in public places where one can take bodies. Maybe fill out a form, or two. You know, name, address and how that body came into your possession. Maybe have separate bins for male and female. But what else is needed?

Let us openly admit it: a body that one does not want and a nearby meat saw is likely to start a certain train of thought in us all. And it turns out, 'cutting up' is the 137th most common way of disposing of a murdered body; not that Sylvia was murdered, but the police are a suspicious lot.

Denis looked at her for the first time in months. She really was quite attractive, although turning a funny colour all over.

He was hungry and those bacon and eggs sounded so good but he was intrigued by the possibility of undressing her. Alcohol always tended to give him an excessive erection next morning. It was a tough decision, but breakfast won, after which he fell asleep and then remembered his Tuesday afternoon lecture. Shower, shave, washing machine, clean clothes, mouthwash and then into the car.

At the University, Denis had trained himself to forget all domestic issues. The workplace often evokes unpretentious joy where worries are entirely rational, whereas home can be a jungle of unexpected terrors: the icy stare, the deafening silences, closed doors, hidden corkscrews, unpaid bills piled by your place at dinner, half-empty bottles of Scotch from last night left on the breakfast table, none of your special cereal left in the packet, your car gone without explanation, a note that it is your turn to pick up the kids from school and don't wait up because your partner is at an office party tonight at the local singles bar.

Finishing his lecture, Denis was reminded that he was leaving on a Geography Field School to Lands End in Cornwall in under an hour and they had already put his travelling bag in the department bus and please to hurry, else they would be travelling half the night.

Denis, like everybody else, mostly slept on the bus, apart from being awoken every few hours for a toilet and roadside snack bar. Eventually, they were at the permanent campsite set up by the Lands End Town Council, and Denis was required to give a talk about the week's domestic and academic arrangements to thirty snoring sleeping bags - some of which seemed to be adopting an internal copulative motion.

Behind Denis were huge cliffs buffeted by crashing waves that had travelled across the North Atlantic to hit the most south-westerly corner of England. Their noise all but drowned out both Denis's instructions and the screaming sleeping bags. The Field School was an escape from reality to a world of daily exploration of rocks and waves. The evenings were a contrived agony of tired bodies trying to write reports and staff talking informally to students without the artificial defensive trappings of the University; the whole thing was designed by a sadistic educational officer, who believed there was no value to be had from a field school without pain.

At the end of the week, Denis finally drove home and remembered his 'little problem'.

In Denis's absence, Rustler had been locked out of the house but had free access to the garage where his feeding bowl stood empty.

Sylvia's fall had left her body broken internally but externally intact, and to Rustler she looked just like one of the carcasses of meat that he could see in the freezer whenever he was allowed into the kitchen. Hunger overtook his body and he decided to visit 'Tom' who was the Golden Retriever living next door, but found that Tom's appetite had already exceeded the contents of his personal bowl, conveniently marked 'Tom', so they collectively visited 'Webster' at number 31.

Pretty soon, three dogs were the nucleus of a pack. Animals, including humans, do things collectively that they would never do alone and Sylvia's body excited their primeval instincts. After a lot of howling, the body was dragged to the top of Smithers Dell whereupon they snarled at one another to find the dominant alpha male who would take the first bite. This developed into a ballet of advancing and retreating dogs pushing against the body causing it to roll down the Dell where it was hit by Denis's returning car.

Police and ambulances arrived with sirens and flashing lights, which added the required sense of emergency to the scene of the accident and gave onlookers the sense that important things were being done to save important lives.

Ten minutes later, the body of one dead woman was taken by ambulance, the body of one golden retriever was dumped in a front garden since its owners were out at the 'Taste of Asia' restaurant. A separate ambulance took Denis, who was unconscious, and a tow truck took his car. Rustler was left standing in the road wondering just what a dog has to do to get a meal, especially now his best friend had gone.

Webster had escaped injury and returned home to number 31. Not a close friend, he had always treated Rustler cordially. Merely putting his nose into Webster's back garden assured Rustler that those days of cordiality were over, and as he turned and ran he heard the shouts of abuse, "That's the dog that started it all," and a stone narrowly missed his right ear and he felt the direct hit of startling cold water from a garden hose.

As he trotted down the Dell, he heard the distant sound of, "Take him to the pound." and then those terrible words that denote human power over all other animals, "best get the little bugger put down."

It is a measure of the ethos of the British middle classes that no one was heard expressing grief for Sylvia.

We all have times in our lives when we know we are not wanted and must move on.

Rustler walked for two days, sometimes hunting in back gardens for food - but he was a domestic dog without hunting skills. Chased by other dogs, he grew thin and weary. When it rained, he drank from puddles and then crawled under hedges where he dreamt of his home with Denis and Sylvia. A cat befriended him and showed him how to find food in a large garbage can at the back of a hotel. Rustler found little that was edible, and then could not get out. After sleeping in the filthy can, he was awakened at dawn by its being emptied into a garbage truck, and now he could not breathe. Clambering through eight feet of rotting trash, he at last found air and could see that the truck was on a highway with other traffic around him. Desperate situations need desperate remedies, and in an act of extreme stupidity, or perhaps extreme bravery, who knows the difference, Rustler thought back to words uttered by Sylvia's mother Magdalena.

The less sensitive of us fail to realise just how high is the intelligence of dogs, and suffice it to say that Rustler had heard Magdalena, expound about the joys of a really good leap.

The occasion had been a Sunday in summer with the traditional tea outside in the back garden. It might even have been somebody's birthday. There were cucumber sandwiches, lemon flavoured iced sponge cake, and strawberries with fresh cream. It was a good tea with lots of bits of cake hurled to Rustler, and he was good enough to bark through the fence and invite 'Tom' from next door to come over to join him.

Rustler was really that sort of dog.

Once satiated with cake, not to mention the occasional cucumber sandwich, the two dogs basked in the dying sun and listened to the conversation about leaping and the general topic of levitation. The dogs imagined themselves flying and leaving all the world's troubles behind. For a start it would be an end to those boring 'walks' were they had to plod round local streets, or, even worse, be taken to the big park near the river and made to recover tennis balls which their stupid owners kept throwing away.

There are times in life when we are all forced to adopt radical solutions to impossible situations and remembering those words of Sylvia's mother, on that beautiful afternoon in the sun, Rustler leaped from the garbage truck.

Car horns screamed as he rolled to the side of the road as if drivers wished to scold him for his lack of adherence to the strict rules set forth in the British Highway Code.

Being just a dog, albeit a very intelligent one, he was unaware of one tiny point regarding the joy of a good leap. It is pretty evident to most of us, but then again we are more advanced in the evolutionary tree, ignoring the fact that we are the mutes who walk behind dogs picking up their poop in plastic bags. Anyway, that tiny point is that Sylvia's mother was, to use a rather technical term, round the bend or in layman's terms totally bloody barmy, or to quote her doctor, 'a real nutcase'.

But how would a dog know that especially when she had been a bishop's wife.

The instant he leaped, Rustler realised that this was surely the end. In that moment, he wished he was a cat with nine lives. For a dog to do such a thing is tantamount to blasphemy in the eyes of all cat and dog lovers and even Rustler regretted that he had so wished and decided to die like a true dog.

Wailing in agony as his body bounced and his head crashed against a curb, he passed out, but just before doing so, Rustler saw a huge black car bearing down on him.

In that moment of dying, or so they say, there is a critical moment when you are not sure whether you are really still alive or have just died.

The car stopped. A man got out, and with great care picked up Rustler in his big arms, "Wow, little feller, what's been happening to *you*. Looks like you need a friend. Let me take you home and get you some food and a bath. Then, a good night's sleep. Okay, excuse me feeling you all over. No, I don't think anything's broken. By the way, let's see who you are."

But Rustler's name and address tag was almost illegible after a week on the road.

"Okay, little matey, I can just about make out *Rust*. I'll call you Rusty. Incidentally, I'm Mike Heron, the comedian."

The Bishop, Comedians, ...

8: A Twenty Stretch

Sylvia's post-mortem showed that she had died five days prior to the car accident from what appeared to be a major fall. The newspapers seized on the photographs of her in bed with Sir Guy Holmes, the whole business of the brothel, 'Flights of Fantasy', her mother's obsession with jumping from windows, and the Bishop's love of sexual dominance, occupied the press for several weeks.

The court accepted that Sylvia died as a result of untreated injuries from a fall from a window. They could not rule on the cause of that fall: whether it was accidental or suicidal. For the sake of comparison, the Court was told that Roy Bolger had fallen at almost the identical spot, but in the middle of a working day, and been found dead on arrival at hospital. Celia Bolger gave evidence that she had been appointed as the official departmental photographer and Sylvia had posed for some rather racy shots for the forthcoming Christmas play. "Yes," she said it was going to be a lot of fun and regretted that Sylvia had not cleared the photographs with Denis. She claimed to be unaware of any unsavoury side to Sylvia's life and thought her a great actress and very photogenic; the man in the photographs was apparently an actor. The photographs were ordered to be confiscated by the court and these were the days when no newspaper would dare disobey a court order. But nevertheless rumours spread and Sir Guy Holmes made a statement that he had been seduced by Mrs Clerk and would set up an annual university prize in her memory to be called the Sylvia

Award worth five thousand pounds. The money seen in the photograph was the first payment. Denis was found guilty of failing to report the accident and obtain emergency medical help. Counsel for the defence claimed that Sylvia was dead on impact and Denis's actions were due to shock. A prison sentence was handed down of only twenty years on the grounds that there were the extenuating circumstances of extreme mental pain caused by the photographs. He was praised for devotion to teaching and his determination to run a geography field school.

Several of the jury, and most of the public, considered Denis not guilty of any crime and felt confident that he would win an Appeal. Because of his standing in the community and this being his first offense, he was sent to Hells Peak Prison, near St Fuller in Cornwall, which is a low-security jail claimed to have a nice view of a wild beach and the incoming Atlantic rollers, seemingly attractive to a geographer.

After Denis was incarcerated, the University Assistant Registrar, Derek Young, who tried to get people to call him 'Dirk', and his friend, Dave, drove over to the 'Willows' and quite by chance met up with a social worker from the Her Majesty's Prison Service charged with the responsibility of settling Denis's affairs. After some discussion with her, Dirk wrote to Denis who agreed to him buying the 'Willows', on condition that the garage was used to store all of Denis's books until his release.

Dirk and Dave, or the double D's as they became humorously known in Telmer St Joseph, were not without their faults, of which the major one was a distinct disinterest in garden maintenance. Their property sloped downwards away from the house into an old, dried-up river creek, and this became filled with weeds and high grasses. When this growth was mentioned by neighbours, Dirk quipped that they preferred to let the land 'go back to nature' and seemed unperturbed that 'nature' would eventually reach their back door.

Importantly, as shall be revealed later in the story, these weeds had hidden beneath them a steel briefcase which had been found in the University parking area the morning after Sylvia's death and sent *Special Delivery* to the 'Willows'. While Denis was still at his Field School at Lands End, Rustler found the briefcase, and thinking it was a large can of dog food, enlisted the help of Tom and Webster to drag it to the bottom of the dell, where it was destined to remain for many years. The steel locks rusted closed and the case became enshrouded in the black, tar-like mud that was characteristic of the district and thought to have been formed deep in the bed of the old river.

Back at Hells Peak Prison, Denis was allowed full privileges. The Governor, Robert King, and the warders, plus the 'consensus of opinion' of the prisoners, considered Denis innocent. He had certainly acted unwisely, but allowance had to be made for the fact that he was an academic, with his head in the clouds, and, moreover, hard pressed for time prior to his geography field school.

On arrival at Hells Gate, he went to Governor King's office and was greeted very warmly, "Denis, just consider this place your home. There's some lovely walking paths roundabout and plenty of nice pubs to wet your whistle while you're out exploring. Think of it this way, Denis: you could be down here in the southwest on convalesce, or on an unexpected holiday. Some of those hotels over there with ocean views would be charging you a fortune. While here you get *free* accommodation and food. Admittedly, our rooms are rather basic, but you'll have one to yourself and I'm sure that you can personalize it as time goes by. Mind you, there's always a chance of an appeal, and we can put your case very forcefully to the review board when they visit us next month. Incidentally, if you are a bird watcher there are some superb spots round here for ornithologists. Feel free to borrow my binoculars. Wonderful views of the beaches."

"Thank you, sir. We are, I assume, just a few miles from Land's End where I have run geography field schools for my students."

"There you are then," said the smiling governor rising his desk and slapping Denis cordially on the back.

"You'll be completely at home here. And, if I may make so bold, professor, you'll have no students to bother you. Please try the Lobster Pot restaurant on the quay at St Fuller. Beautiful food. All so fresh, you know. Straight out of the sea. And, I gather that your financial affairs are in good order. So, no problem there."

Denis was exhausted after the last months, but slowly adapted to prison life and there was little chance of his being lonely as every man in his block stopped to talk about his case. He explained over and over again that his wife had simply gone out the window. Admitting to being confused at the time, he now realised that suspicion would be directed towards him. And, yes, he had been extremely silly, but he hoped that the tabloids would force the court to look at his case again.

After a week, he thought that he might as well start to explore the countryside and stretch his legs. The warder on his floor told him that prisoners with special privileges were allowed to change into civilian clothes and leave for periods of up to six hours. An identity pass would be needed, signed by Governor King, and that would need renewing each month. The warder filled out some forms and guessed they should all be back in a couple of days and, in the meantime, Denis should have a set of photographs taken in the prison office.

After almost a week, his daily freedom pass had not been issued by Governor King's office, and he asked the warder for help.

"I don't rightly know, Clerk. I'll make some inquiries. It's probably just sitting on his desk. But mind you, the word around us *screws* here --."

"--Screws?"

"Sorry, yes *screws*, that's what the inmates calls us. Yes, we *screws* reckon that Robert King is looking for a bit of personal publicity in the way you're treated here, and as soon as you gets out, what will be just a few weeks, you can help him with a bit of promotion to a more prestigious prison. You are, after all, a member of some important committees."

"Well, I *was*, yes. Not sure I will be *ever again*."

When Denis had first arrived at Hells Peak, Governor King had been happy to be addressed as Robert, but never by the diminutives, Rob or Bob.

Gossip in the prison shower block, where such things as personal size were a frequent topic of conversation, even demonstration, indicated that since Robert King was a rather short man, his genitalia were presumably suitably scaled down, and he needed all the extra length implicit in the use of the full length 'Robert'.

But that was just the stuff of prison ablution blocks which we are all advised to ignore.

Denis had written several textbooks and thought that he could spend his time at Hells Peak writing some more. Most especially, he wanted to finish 'Introduction to Numerical Spatial Analysis', which had rested on his university desk for the last three years, along with monthly reminders from his publishers. He would need a typewriter and some of his reference books, but supposed that was just a formality to be cleared with Robert King.

He was wrong.

Slowly, the Sunday tabloids became filled with stories about some of the cruel pranks that had been perpetrated at Oxenbridge. Then, they dug up stories about Sylvia's mother and the 'Bishop of the Red Light District'.

It is hard to overestimate the value of Denis's case as a gift to the tabloids, and Robert King began to see that he could earn himself some publicity by ensuring that Denis was properly punished.

Seeing Governor King in the prison exercise yard, Denis took the opportunity to ask him about his daily freedom pass, his books, and typewriter.

There was a terrible change in King's attitude.

Looking up at Denis, he sneered, "You listen here Clerk. I've been reading about some of your goings-on, mate. You're here for punishment, and it's punishment that you'll get. Make no mistake about *that*. You were the head of a university department from hell, with murder and deceit your middle name."

"But Robert, you authorised daily freedom for me, even borrowing your binoculars. Please don't believe that rubbish in the tabloid --."

"Don't you dare address me in that fashion, Clerk. First year here, you have no privileges. Plus, you're to have extra duties scrubbing out the lavatory block twice weekly with a tooth brush."

"*Robert*, what are you saying? You can't mean it."

"You will have no books or paper, and you are forbidden to write. You are here to be punished for *murder*."

"But, I didn't do it."

"And Clerk, you call me *sir*, else I'll know the reason why. I gather from the 'News of Britain' edition last Sunday that you caused Dr Roy Bolger to die through your plotting and scheming. Then sent your wife to work as a whore to further your little aims. You bloody murdered her. She, being the daughter of an insane woman who was regularly raped by the Bishop of Gostchester. Bet you organized that as well. Get the hell out of my way, you piece of filth. I'll make you wish you were never born."

In terms of traditional romantic fiction, Denis had made a *bad* marriage. It was the sort of thing that all sons used to be warned about by their mothers. Yet despite those warnings, intelligent men keep making those mistakes. In fact the more intelligent they are, the greater their vulnerability.

I expect you have heard the warnings countless times about how girls are so scheming and devious. Had

Denis just married the girl next door in Clover Creek where he was born, he could have enjoyed a comfortable easy life and perhaps been blessed with many rosy cheeked children. His father's butchery business was there for the asking, and a leg of New Zealand lamb can be a joy in its own right. Given some local mint sauce, there is really nothing left to want in this world. There was nothing much left for Denis to lean about butchery and, ever since he was a small boy, he knew all the tricks of the trade. Before he went to school each morning, he could morph a fully grown lamb into a set of joints for sale, plus a neat set of choice offal.

Without Sylvia, he would admittedly never have become a professor in a fifth rate British university and written books on spatial analysis, but that is really something we can all do without: the last words of academics on their death beds is rarely, "Oh shit, I do wish I had written one more text book on spatial analysis."

As the reality of his 20 year imprisonment struck, Denis fell into deep depression, and Governor King's remedy was an instruction to his warders to use their boots to kick him into a more submissive frame of mind.

This continued for two years.

Slowly Denis's mind decayed to the point that he was close to becoming an imbecile. Monthly medical inspections by the peripatetic prison medical service showed that he was in the early stages of senile dementia and was henceforth restricted to light duties in the prison kitchen, where he was known as the Mad Prof, and given the job of sawing up the raw meat carcasses.

"We gather Clerk that you had a meat saw in your garage," was the humorous daily chant of the warders. In their ignorance, the other prisoners were actually being kind and Denis's mind found solace in those memories of youth.

It is worthwhile for us to consider that Denis did have a means of escaping this murder rap altogether. Let us think back to the night that Sylvia went out the window in his office. It is a far guess that nobody had seen her arrive at the University at 6pm. Or if they had, there would be no memory. There was absolutely nobody but Denis in the Geography Department. As for other people on campus, would anybody have the slightest recall?

True her body was laying in the parking area for five to ten minutes but Denis had scooped it into his car just before the security guard made his rounds.

So Denis got her body into his garage before it was ever seen. He had an electric meat saw built for cutting up sheep and there was nobody else home to complain about the noise. Plus, I need you to be aware reader, that Denis was very experienced and had helped his old dad cut up carcases since he was a boy. There are of course lots of trade secrets and Denis had brought back with him from New Zealand, along with the saw, several cans of what his father called 'butcher's friend'. I am not going to give away any secrets by telling you what is in this powder but suffice it to saw it stops blood splattering everywhere.

Working with reasonable speed, Sylvia's body could have been reduced to three large plastic bags in less than an hour. In fact this technique is commonplace for the US Mafia, and 'Slaughter House Borazonio' in New

Jersey holds the US record for Human Corpse to Bags of twenty -seven minutes.

A word of advice here is that disposal is often a problem. Many an operator has been caught out by a trail of blood leaking from his car as he parked it on a high river bridge waiting for the passing traffic to clear. But Denis had none of those potential pitfalls: at the bottom of his garden lay a steep slope leading into the caverns of the earth. He could have been all cleaned up, relaxed, feet up, enjoying some very cold Kiwi beer inside two hours.

"What about Sylvia?" I hear you ask. "Surely people will miss her."

Well she could have gone for her weekend of shame with Sir guy and just never been heard of again. We would feel fairly sorry for Denis, but let us admit the truth, it would probably be for the best.

But all that did not happen, but it was certainly a fantasy that grew in Denis's mind with time. He calmed himself with the thought that innocent men do not dismember bodies. Mike Heron had once written an essay for Mr Oliver in which a passenger in a train sees a spare leg hanging out of a luggage rack and comments astutely, "A spare leg is definite proof of foul play and we are not talking chickens here." So we must always remember that Denis was totally innocent, though ill advised. Nevertheless, he was innocent.

When not working in the kitchens, Denis sat in his cell and stared at the floor, or lay on his bunk and stared at the ceiling. No visitors came. Sylvia was dead, and no one from Oxenbridge was likely to visit him.

Then, out of the blue, a retired geographer named Roger Stringer showed up one visiting day. Roger had known Denis slightly when he was first appointed at Oxenbridge. They sat either side of a small table in a room filled with similar tables that were mostly occupied by prisoners and their wives. Roger seemed to have little interest in Denis's plight, and mainly wanted to boast about the orchard that he'd just bought near Saunders Bonk in Somerset with money inherited after his father's death in Canada.

Mainly interested in looking at his fellow prisoners' wives, Denis became aware of his own sexual frustrations. There is a convention in British prisons that all prisoners are allowed what is euphemistically called 'personal time', usually on a Saturday afternoon, where they can be undisturbed in their cells. It is intended to allow them to relieve their sexual needs and then enjoy the post-orgasmic sleep.

As Denis looked around at the prisoner's wives, he wondered whether he would remarry when he was eventually released. Was that possible, and did he even want another woman in his life? Sylvia had brought such pain and now sentenced him to twenty years of utter misery. When released, he would be an old, broken man. Gradually, he came to hate her, and realised that he was happier to accept the lie that he *had* murdered her. That realization felt good. Mouthing the words, 'bloody bitch' felt so good. It is often easier to accept a lie than convince others of the truth, and Denis had reached that point.

Roger was talking about his apples, but read Denis's lips and responded, "She was a bitch alright, Denis. You did the right thing. Never thought that you had it in you."

"Nor me, Rog. But I certainly got rid of the bloody witch."

The room was silent. All eyes were on Denis. Even the warders stood still, watching and listening.

"I did the right thing. I did what was *right*."

His words were spread across every tabloid in the world. Several of the warders bought new cars. From then on, Denis was treated kindly by all the other prisoners. The Board of Review gave Robert King a very severe rap over the knuckles for his lack of care of Denis during his early days in the prison, and he was demoted to the rank of Night Warder and relocated to an isolated prison for violent criminals on the Scottish moors, where he was always known as 'Wee Bobbie'.

With Denis at last settled into his confinement, although entirely unjustly, because he is an innocent man, we will leave him temporarily and head off to look at events in the lives of two sisters, Kaye and Claudia Fortie who are to be critical to our story.

9: Kaye Fortie

Pushing the knob on the car's CD player produced the wonderful sounds of 'Nights in White Satin' sung by Justin Hayward of the Moody Blues. It transformed Kaye Fortie to another world of real love and beauty where the night was her rescuer and would take her away from all this absurd drudgery and the pathetically menial nature of her life as a typist. Surely the almighty had meant her for something better than typing out invoices. But at least she had a job and an apartment with rent which she could afford.

She needed now to make her dinner. It had been a hard day. Leaving her car in her allotted parking space, Kaye let the romantic music fade in her mind and faced the reality of life. Exhausted and tense, she pulled leftovers from the freezer.

"Oh, that's bloody cold," Kaye shrieked, tossing it into the air to keep her hands from freezing.

The plastic package looked like the chicken casserole that she had made last month. Or, alternatively, it might be the rabbit stew from Easter. No matter, she pushed it into her little ceramic bowl, still dirty on the sink, and looked for the defrost button on the microwave. It would take twenty minutes.

"That's bloody ridiculous. Twenty minutes? What's in the fridge? I'm sooooo hungry."

White wine stared back at her from the fridge. The bottle was tinted green and glowed in the interior fridge lights so as to convey the goodness of nature. Wine bottles are at their most alluring when nearly, but not quite, full. The bottle gave Kaye a message of reassurance that a single glass would be quite acceptable and to be enjoyed whilst she waited for the 'defrost'. Tempting indeed. But, after she had passed out on the floor last Saturday, she had promised herself that she would wait until Friday for a drink.

It had been a dispiriting experience, waking with the full morning sun in her eyes. Her first thought had been, "Oh shit, please tell me that I didn't leave the gas on in the kitchen."

She had.

It was a saucepan of *chili concarne,* which was now a thick black glue at the bottom of the pan.

"Bloody hell."

It had burnt her hand, even through the oven glove and a tea towel.

"Shit," as her face was hit by the steam from the tape.

"Oh no, is that blood?"

There had been a gash on her right forearm, and in the sitting room she had found broken glass and the base of a wine glass.

"Please say that I didn't start on that bottle of Irish Cream Brandy."

She found the bottle empty on the couch.

"That was all *then*, and now is *now*," she rationalized, assuring herself that tonight she would resist that bottle of white wine.

Still fifteen minutes to go on the 'defrost'.

Turn on the TV.

Oh no, not that again. On the screen before her, Kaye was viewing a repeat of that terrible Mike Heron Show from last Friday. Bad enough having it once a week, but now her indignation was once again ignited by the temerity of BritishTV in repeating such an outright exploitation of women on the next Thursday.

"That man Heron really annoys me. His show is so disrespectful to women. Does he think that we're living in the 1930's?"

She watched as a clown ran across the screen chasing a girl in heels, her full skirt blowing up to expose hosiery and underwear.

"Bloody hell, this is disgraceful. Where's the phone?"

The BritishTV complaint number was on her fast dial. Her policy was to complain about any show that dishonoured women and to report it to an organisation which she had helped start called WOW-LASSIE, which was an acronym for 'Women Of the World League Against Sex and Sexism In Entertainment'.

The Microwave peeped.

It *was* the rabbit casserole.

"Oh, shit, I can't possibly eat rabbit casserole without red wine. Oh bugger, I'm sounding exactly like Rick. Bloody shithouse of a man."

The rabbit casserole was still half frozen and yet truly cremated around the edges. How was that possible? Bloody Rick had cooked it, sod him. Calling "ashes to ashes," she committed the rabbit to the white plastic waste bin.

They had gone to the open-air farmers market early on Easter Sunday morning, after making love in her single bed on Saturday night. She invented a new word to describe his oral skills: technicious. But she refused to use her mouth on his genitals. It was disgusting, and degraded her as a woman. No amount of persuasion by sister Claudia wound change her mind.

"Kaye darling, it's a wonderful feeling as you control their orgasm and make them wait to unleash all that warm creamy fluid into your mouth."

In Britain in the 1970's, the traditional end to a Saturday night's romp was to stay together on the Sunday and make an early evening meal followed by, "Sorry, I have to go. I've got a really early morning ahead and hell of a week," and the expected response, "Me too. Look, it was lovely. Are you going to be at the Collingbrook Summer Party?"

"It's usually such a blast, but --."

It was all a lie of course and part of the pantomime of living in Britain in the 60's and 70's in which young people pretended to be part of a wild, careless society recovering from war.

That Sunday morning, they had wrapped arms around one another at the butchers stall, which she thought disgusting, but was suitably impressed with his handling of the line of hanging rabbits.

"I'll have it skinned and cleaned for yer, governor, in free minutes. Pop over to Mrs Clive and get yer-selves cups of 'ot steaming cha."

Rick poured whiskey into their thickly stewed, hot, sweet tea from a hip flask shaped like her memories of his bum, and she noticed in the bright morning sunshine, the flagging, aging skin round his neck. He must be ten years older than he claimed.

The tea was sweet and slightly intoxicating in contrast to her normal breakfast of half a grapefruit;

the eating of this bitter fruit each morning is something of a sacred duty for the English and is such a challenge that the rest of the day seems relatively easy.

"Peep, peep," the microwave yawned.

The casserole was inedible.

Claiming a period starting that Sunday afternoon, she had donned heavy jeans and ragged sweater with high collar, and they lay on the floor pretending to enjoy the Sunday papers. Laughing at the reviews of London plays, he burst out "Oh darling, I saw that one in its pre-West End run in Brighton when I needed to break the boredom of a second night with mater and pops." Was he really homosexual? In retaliation, she feigned enjoyment of the article on the new exhibition at The Tate, spouting off as if she knew lots about the Post-Van Smit School of Dutch Indonesian Art.

He'd left at five in the afternoon with, "Got to dash Kaye. Suggest you freeze the left-overs. Defrost slowly; add a glass of *something red*. Really cheap and rough, and then stick it in oven at 350 for twenty minutes. Blob of yogurt on top, a stick of French bread, and Bob's your uncle. On no account, use the microwave, darling. Okay, Kaye?"

He thought he was so cute when he made fun of her name like that.

"Sod off, you arrogant bastard," she muttered to the memory of his very aristocratic looking cock with a sort of bend in the middle and tapering to a blunt head.

"You can always tell," Claudia had warned with her vast range of sexual experiences, "where their cock has been."

Kaye steamed with anger about his condescending way of talking about cooking as if she knew nothing. It was supposed to endear him as a man in touch with his emotions. Just ten years ago he would have been labelled 'queer', but now it was supposed to be a great attraction for women. That, plus his beard pushing across the mound of Venus.

The first time they made love, she sort of came. More like a pain, or tension, that relieved itself with some wishy-washy blue sparkly lights as if there were a volume knob somewhere that needed turning up. She screamed politely, mainly to make him stop. On that Sunday, he didn't really seem to care and she did a rather comical fake which she and her sister Claudia had perfected some years ago while sitting in a rather dreary restaurant in London's Soho.

"You're got to learn to quiver, Kaye." Claudia professed such worldly knowledge of sex. "And let your excitement come up to a crescendo. Men are always impressed if you squeeze your nipples at the same time. Got to decide whether you internalise your orgasm and just let out a long sigh, or whether you are a shouter and the people next door call the fire brigade."

By that stage, the rather dreary restaurant was filled with gaping jawed men of the type one finds in Soho just wandering about haplessly.

Claudia continued, "Those cries are important to men and really bring on their erection. That's why the silly buggers go to dirty movies here in Soho to watch women having sex. And that's why, to men, sex is a spectator sport."

What could she eat? There was a bit of cold ham in the fridge. She pulled out a slice from the plastic package and tested it under her nose. It smelt of nothing despite its claim to have been roasted on oak logs during a Bavarian winter. Was that the price? How could she been so stupid? Why was it so wet and slippery?

There was a cut loaf with only two, rather curled-up, slices left which she put on a plate, and looked for the butter. It was hard as a rock. Into the microwave with it, and push the 'One Minute Express' button.

"Need to watch it. Damn it's the phone."

"Thank you for your complaint about one of our programs. Your reference number is 866521997. Please feel free to contact BritishTV at any time."

Peep, peep.

Picking up the plastic container of butter with the oven glove, she poured the yellow liquid onto her two slices of curly bread. One slice did a sort of double somersault onto the floor and the other demonstrated that stale bread has limited absorbency for any fluid. A yellow river dripped from plate to countertop.

"SOD that Mike Heron," Kaye screamed, obviously reaching the end of the proverbial rope.

Why couldn't they have programs on TV where decent working girls, like herself, chased naked men across fields and over fences? Yes, over fences covered with barbed wire. Lots of close-ups.

Images of spikes in delicate places.

She needed the toilet.

Why not get into her pyjamas and have just one glass of that white wine.

Okay, take it with her now to the bathroom.

Oh boy, that tasted so good. Just what I needed. Another look at the bottle in case she needed a second glass. Oh good, there was plenty, and yes, a second bottle in the cupboard. Might as well put it in the freezer, just in case. She wasn't going to drink it but just so as to be prepared.

The phone again.

Who the hell could that be, at this time, on a Thursday?

"Hi Kaye, darling"

It was her sister.

"Claudia, how lovely. It's been ages."

"Sorry to be so late Kaye but, well, something's come up. Or rather, not come up, as it were."

"Oh Lor, Claudia, is something wrong? Nothing wrong with Mummy, I hope?"

"No. I've had a bit of luck. I'm really over the moon."

"What is it? Not the lottery. No, that doesn't come out til Saturday night."

"No darling. It's Ryan."

"What?"

"He left me."

"Claudia, you must be joking. No? Well, that *is news*. It's a shock, really."

"Kaye, I'm on cloud nine. Not that it's much of a surprise."

"Well you could have fooled me. You two seemed so happy together."

"No, darling Kaye. It's been on the outs for months. We haven't had a decent screw this year, and he's been getting it somewhere. When you do a man's laundry, there are tell-tale signs. Plus he's been on his best behaviour. You know, putting the lid down on the toilet and everything. Not leaving pee all over the floor."

"Look Claudia it's kind of late. Can we get together for a coffee at the weekend and talk it through. I'm sure that it'll all blow over. Sorry 'blow' is a bad word. I meant you'll be back together in a week. He really loves you, you know."

"No time, darling Kaye. That's why I phoned now. The point is that I would like you to come with me to Malta on Saturday?"

"*What*?" Kaye exclaimed, nearly dropping the phone. Recovering her composition, "Of course, I *vaguely* remember now. You told me that you two might go to Malta."

"One of those short breaks they advertise, darling. You know pictures of a perfect couple under a blue sky with a hunk in tight bathers, and a blonde who is all boobs, sipping long cool drinks against a background of sea and enormous sun umbrellas."

"So you actually went ahead and booked?"

"That's right. I'd booked for me and Ryan, so you can now take his place. All I need to do is pay a ten-pound transfer fee. The whole package was hundreds, and I hate to waste it. Plus it will do us both good, I'm sure."

"I can't just drop everything and just go, Claudia. I mean I do have enough leave from work, but I can't just go at a moment's notice."

"*Why not*? Come on, Kaye, it's only ten days, and your work will still be there when you come back. Typing invoices is not exactly time-sensitive stuff."

"Brookes, my boss will never agree. And, I know what you're going to say. I will not do that. It demeans not just me but all women."

She used her short black skirt, and answered Brooke's questions about where his wife could get a pair of heels that high.

Male eyes followed her to her desk, and she was glad of the modesty board in front of her legs. Almost immediately she needed the bathroom. She listened from her stall to girls talking about their men.

"That Mike Heron Show will be on tonight. Gets him so randy. I had to put on that stupid garter belt and those French knickers. Why are men like that? But it does mean we get some fun on a Friday night. We're just sex objects, but, hey, *who cares*."

"I do," muttered Kaye. Suddenly, she couldn't wait to leave. Okay, he has agreed that I could go at lunchtime. I'll just slip out the back way *now*."

10: Malta

The queue at Malta Immigration was long. Tourists stood in a line along a fence across a sun baked airfield and took off coats and jackets. Occasionally people walked past along the other side of the fence having gone through passport control.

Claudia took off first her heels and then her hosiery and croaked, "Wow, this heat is unbelievable. My clothes are stuck to me." A small dark man was walking along the line selling cold drinks from a cart, and tourists were opening their duty-free liquor to add to cans of coke and lemonade. "First time I ever had hot vodka and lemon," swigged a man ahead of them. And then he added to Claudia, "You girls here alone? It's my tenth time. Come every summer. Got a tiny villa in Gozo."

"Oh, really. Actually, can you tell us how to get to Gozo from here?"

"Certainly. Just hop in a taxi and go down to the ferry. I'm going that way, myself. You're welcome to come with me, if you like."

"How often do the ferries run?"

"Next one is," and he looked at his watch, "let me see, it'll be the six o'clock."

"Oh Lor," Kaye groaned as she opened her bottle of whiskey. It was already warm, and she took a hearty swig that set off a cough. It was the same cough that seemed always to accompany her periods.

Then she felt blood on her leg.

"*What*, I'm bleeding. Not my period already. Oh no."

Her mother had told her that once her cycles became irregular, she would go into menopause quite quickly, citing their family history, "Kaye, I started when I was only thirty nine, and *my mother* got it all over before she was thirty five. Good job, I say. Who wants that bloody mess every month?"

Claudia fished out some pads and tissues that she carried for emergencies and, handing them to Kaye, advised her to find a ladies room, promising to keep their place in the line. Upon her return, they took some swigs from Kaye's bottle.

"If only men had to put up with this every month," Kaye moaned, "they would understand a bit more about the world. Bet that Mike Heron isn't even married."

"Bloody bastard."

"You know Mike?" came the response from a person who had stopped on the other side of the wire fence, "Because what you just said doesn't seem quite fair."

"Oh, *it doesn't seem quite fair*," taunted Claudia. "Well, bugger me. Excuse us for believing he's a sodding male, chauvinist pig."

Kaye took another swig and sighed "Sod it, we have five hours to wait in this heat until we get to the ferry, and I suppose we'll have to get some bloody bus or something."

Kaye looked across the fence to see rather rumpled clothes, peaked cloth cap, and backpack. There was something rather familiar about this person's demeanour and the sound of their voice.

What was it?

Something on TV?

The person pointed towards a row of taxis, "Don't worry there are plenty of taxis, down at the gate," came the voice again, "and a nice restaurant by the ferry."

It was so familiar and yet so distant. Determined to pin down the voice, Kaye smiled, "By the way, I'm Kaye Fortie. Sorry for the remarks about Mike Heron. I'm a member of WOW LASSIE."

But her efforts were in vain as the crumpled figure looked aghast and hastened off to the gate where she boarded a taxi.

The queue for Immigration was not moving, and as they sat on the ground Claudia sensed that Kaye was experiencing huge doubts about this journey.

Marshalling her sisterly influence, "But, Kaye, it's a really nice hotel when we get there. Ryan picked it out from the brochure. It overlooks Ramla Beach, which is spectacular. Look, here's a picture."

As Claudia pulled the brochure from her bag, a multitude of personabilia spilled across the path, and a wicked little afternoon breeze from the sea decided to liven up its day by blowing the fallout in a myriad of directions. As Kaye and Claudia scampered to retrieve them, the queue suddenly started moving, and after ten minutes of collecting just about everything they could find, they realised that they were now at the end of the line. At two o'clock, a passport officer came out yawning and told the ten remaining people in the line that the officers were going for siesta, and Immigration would re-open in an hour.

"Sod that," fumed Claudia, and they pushed their way aggressively ahead, stepping over passport officers asleep on the floor, and into the vacant customs hall where their checked-luggage stood forlorn and abandoned. There were no taxis, and, in answer to their query, a policeman volunteered, "They all gone to hotels. More here in evening."

"Where the *hell* is that fellow who was in the line?" Kaye groaned. "Whatever made me agree to come on this escapade? To think I could be home all nice and comfy on a Saturday afternoon, watching TV and planning my dinner."

11: Male World

As a child, Kaye would play endlessly alongside her sister Claudia, and the days would pass one after the other. Then, suddenly, adulthood was upon her, and she realised that although she was an adult, the greater reality was that she was a woman in a man's world. Going to buy a car and asking for finance, "We'll need your husband's signature, dear. Oh, okay you're not married. That's fine, just get your dad to sign the agreement. Your dad died of TB? Not sure what you can do, love. Perhaps time to get married. You're a good looking girl so it shouldn't be difficult."

Her first room in London. "I'll rent you the room love, but no men, okay? You start bringing men in 'ere and yer owt on yer ear. I wants three months in advance."

The men at work watching her.

Her report on the Sunderland Coalmine collapse. She had worked two weekends and every evening until one in the morning on that report. Her job was at Fulham Technical Consultancies, which had been looking to employ an experienced engineer.

"You are hardly *that*," she was told disdainfully at her interview. "But if you are able to work with our technical director as more or less a – cough, cough -- clerical assistant, it should be possible for us to take you on at a much reduced wage."

Her pay was just about enough for the rent and a meagre diet of canned food cooked over the single gas ring.

"Look Kaye. Need to talk to you about this report of yours on the Sunderland Coalmine. Okay. Let me say up front, it's damn good."

Brian Jackson, shifted uneasily in his hard wooden desk chair.

"I've no complaints with the report."

Brian was head of the company's technical section and it was the first time she had met him in person. Smiling back at him in just the way she did at school when the teacher complimented her homework, she crossed her legs and was surprised when he blushed.

She had been raised by her parents to believe that the greatest attribute one can have in life is the ability to think.

"Doesn't matter what you know, girls," her father had pontificated every morning over breakfast. "Important thing is to be able to think things through and do research."

To that end, he had bought a copy of 'Encyclopaedia Britannica' which consisted of 45 volumes of information written by the world's experts on every topic known to the human race. When he died, Claudia had told Kaye that she could have 'the dammed thing'.

"It's been sitting in the front room," she had scowled, "for ten years looking at me in judgment."

But for Kaye, the encyclopaedia was a window to the world. And, starting at age eight, she had methodically read it, starting at volume 1. By the time she moved to her job at Fulham Technical Consultancies she was on volume 13. Her father had signed up for the annual updates and so the original 45 volumes had now grown to 55. The cost of carting these volumes to London had strained her available cash resources, but Volume Ma - Mt had yielded all she needed to know about mining disasters when supplemented with weekends searching back copies of The Times Newspaper at the London Reference Library.

The blush had disappeared from Brian's face and, as if embarrassed by himself, he strutted back and forth across his dismal office with hands deep in pockets. Seeming to be playing with something in his right hand, Kaye politely assumed it was his keys although Claudia had once told her about a bad habit that some men develop when under stress.

"Who wrote this report Kaye? I want the truth, mind. No girl could do this. Who's your boyfriend? Got yer into bed did he, in exchange for this report? Sounds a bit like that bloody bright spark, Peter Erho to me, at International Mining Systems."

Shaking her head in disbelief, "I wrote that report myself. Who was that man you mentioned, Peter Er-- who?"

"Don't try those tricks with me, girl. But I am going to use the report. I don't care if you had to put out to get it written. I know all the tricks. Don't you try teaching new tricks to an old dog. Hope that you're not bloody pregnant. But that's your problem. Not our's."

He laughed smugly knowing the terrible fate which would await Kaye if she were pregnant.

"Pregnant? I have no idea what you mean, sir."

"But the report is good and will mean a lot of money to be paid out to the coal miners. But I need a name on the report. So I'll use my own. Make it easier. But I'm going to have to dismiss you."

"What? *Why*?"

"Because my dear girl, it's such a bloody cheek saying that *you* wrote it. Why, there's words in 'ere that even I had to look up and you just a slip of a girl. You go back to yer desk and pack yer things and be gone."

As she left, he called after her, "By the way, better not ask me for a reference else I'll say that you are a cheat. My advice for getting a job is to raise that skirt ten inches."

Without a reference, she became a secretary and took that ten inches advice. Brian left FTC soon after her and worked as a private consultant. His first, and only, commission was the company who owned the Sunderland mine that had collapsed, after which he retired to a nice villa in Spain.

After the debacle at FTC, Kaye's next boss was Mark who owned the Sloane Street Investment Bank. Employed as his secretary, Kaye was at the Bank for six whole weeks before he even came into the office. The senior partner at the bank had shown her to her desk on the day that she started work and told her to just answer the phone until Mark appeared. "And also, Miss Fortie, please keep up his appointments book. It's there on his desk."

The book was empty and his phone never rang. So she sat and stared out the window at the building opposite which was a hotel next to the London Stock Exchange. At midday she went out to buy lunch which was a pickled egg and glass of shandy at a very crowded pub. Next day she abandoned the short skirt and wore pants.

Occasionally, faces, conditioned to disappointment, would mutter at the door, "Mark?" and she would shake her head. Feeling she was in solitary confinement, Kaye would sometimes wander down from Mark's penthouse office to the working floors of the bank but was always stopped by security guards and told that she should be on the top floor.

People left to their own devices for long periods do strange things and after she found herself playing noughts and crosses in the condensation from her breath on the cold office window, Kaye decided to create a personal project. Thinking of the Mike Heron Show her mind conceived a plan to outlaw sexual exploitation on TV. In the coming weeks she phoned many women and discussed her idea and thus was born WOW-LASSIE, the Women of the World's League Against Sex and Sexism In Entertainment. In fact it was not just entertainment where women were both sex objects and slaves but Kaye could hear her father's dictum of 'one thing at a time'.

Then, one Friday afternoon, three months later, Mark appeared saying, "Just popped in to see if you could --. Just a moment, you're not *Muriel*."

"No, I think sir that Muriel resigned. Ages ago. I'm Kaye, your new secretary. I've been here months."

"Good lord, really. Well, how are you? I mean, nice to meet you. Look, I have to go to a Banker's dinner tonight and, basically, Muriel was always on hand to fill in as my – *companion* – you know what the Americans would call my formal-- *date*. Can't really go alone to these command performances. She used to keep all her evening and cocktail dresses in that tall cupboard over there."

But the cupboard was bare.

"Look, what was your name again, yes, 'Kaye', that's it, sorry 'bout this, but it's kind of part of the job really. But you weren't to know. I say, if I give you some cash?"

Mark picked up the phone, and five minutes later a clerk entered with a thousand pounds in cash by which time Mark had left saying over his shoulder, "Savoy, seven-thirty for eight."

Kaye continued working on her own project and then left for home at her normal time of 5 pm.

Three weeks later Mark appeared once more on a Friday afternoon, and, as he did so, Kaye handed him her resignation dated three weeks earlier along with the thousand pounds and announced, "Sir, I was hired as a secretary, not an escort or social manager."

As it was the last Friday night in the month, Kaye headed to Euston Station and took a train home to see her mother for the weekend. When she arrived, there was a black BMW sports car in the drive and Mark was lounging on the sofa, sharing a bottle of sherry with her mother.

Standing, he nodded, "Sorry," at Kaye, adding, "had yer home address, and phone number, from your original application letter. So Mum told me that you were on yer way. I want you to reconsider your resignation, and I want to be friends. I must *bugger off* now, but I will be at work Monday and would like to take you down into the bank proper to meet everybody. Need your help with some new plans for modernization."

That was the start of a love affair, and she had been as happy as at any time in her life. Mark was a shy lover and asked for her guidance in all things. Love changes our body's chemistry and produces a sense of wellbeing that transforms everything. Kaye was in love, and even just thinking about Mark made her breathless. He stayed in town for weeks on end and they made love with passion and without restraint in his London flat. They never went to the Bank. On the few occasions that Mark needed to attend an official social occasion, he would simply phone his cousin, the Hon Pamela Horsham-Goodwin. "No point in your getting dressed up, Kaye. I won't be more than a few hours, darling. I'll bring you back a nice piece of cake."

They had been so happy, and one weekend went to meet his parents. His mother asked if she was pregnant.

"We'll need a male heir, yer know. I want you to go by the name Elizabeth. Much more becoming to the family. *Kaye* sounds like half a slang affirmative. Never do. Mark's in the City, of course. I don't approve. Should be running the Estate, plus a bit of hunting and fishing down here. Nothing wrong with a few days at his Club, of course. But there we are. You'll be mistress of his London flat in The Strand."

"What the bloody hell do you mean by hitch hiking home, Kaye?" Mark stormed at her in the office on Monday morning. "Just walking out like that in the middle of the night. Mother was in a rage. Made me feel an utter, bloody fool."

"Oh dear. Made you feel a fool did she. What about me, you bloody useless piece of shit. Sorry, *old boy*. I'm not for sale. Go stuff your family home, and all your money, right up your jacksie."

His face was a pallid white, a shade seen only in the faces of the British Gentry.

12: Knight in White

Let us return to Malta, where Kaye and Claudia are en route to the ferry for Gozo.

The bus was crowded with tourists and workers who commuted daily from Gozo to Malta. Kaye was now fairly well down her bottle of whiskey and needed a bathroom. They bought their tickets at the ferry port and were then told that the ferry would be late because of the storm that was coming across the Mediterranean from Sicily.

According to the Maltese, everything that is bad in life comes from either 'Sicily' or 'Africa'. The approaching storm was coming in from the West, and its precursor had been the mischievous little breeze that had played 'catch-me-if-you-can' with Claudia's papers at the Airport.

Expecting a two-hour wait for the evening boat, they poured themselves into plastic chairs which scrapped and juddered on the concrete balcony of 'The Ferry Inn' and told the waiter to bring drinks which were, "Very cold and very alcoholic."

"Kaye, there's blood on your leg. Are those the shorts you bought when we went to *Belladorme* two years ago?"

The waiter flicked dark, Mediterranean eyes at Kaye and asked to be paid immediately for the drinks.

"I don't get this bill," groaned Claudia squinting through sunglasses at the bill. "I'm not doing detailed conversions from Maltese pounds to British pounds. All right. Can't be bothered. So I'm working on it being two of their's to one of ours. In that case this is going to be a bloody cheap holiday. Hang on, that's weird. I changed two hundred pounds at London Airport and they only gave me one hundred instead of four, or whatever."

Kaye tripped as she ran for stairs beside a notice bearing the internationally accepted sign for a female toilet which is a figure with a symbolic triangular skirt.

"I hate that sodding sign," Kaye yelled as her right knee hit the first step.

"Why so," came a soft English voice, and she felt strong hands lift her from the waist and slide upward under her armpits.

"There is a lot of blood on your leg, madam."

He was dressed in a beautifully tailored white suit with a white hat and dashing waves of fair hair with immense sunglasses.

"I'd better take you down to my yacht and attend to some of your wounds."

Kaye had waited most of her life for the appearance of such an alpha male who would sweep away all worries and concerns.

The dizziness of the hot sun seemed like paradise as he put his right arm under her knees, his left arm under her shoulders and carried her off around the curve of a wall that lead to more steps, but this time, steps down to the harbour.

Relaxing in his arms produced a sensation close to the pre-orgasmic chills she had felt when, as a young girl, she had kissed the boy next door.

Claudia stood and shouted, but Kaye merely waved back to her with, "You go on to Gozo. I'll catch you up in a day or so."

"Kaye, be careful, darling. Remember you hate men."

"Sorry, darling, can't hear you."

Secure in her rescuer's arms, Kaye breathed the intoxicating scent of aftershave and realised that her life was about to enter the glamorous world that she had seen on TV commercials.

His, "Ahoy there," brought a launch out from one of the big yachts, manned by two sailors dressed in white pants with blue-and-white striped nautical shirts. They took Kaye from his arms and put a towel around her leg and then noticed more blood on the other leg.

"Sorry guys," she admitted with feminine embarrassment, I seem to be in full stream."

As they reached the yacht, her white knight hopped aboard and called over his shoulder, "Welcome to my little tub. I called it *Wandering Cloud*. I have some immediate clownish business. See you at dinner. Shower and get some rest for a few hours and then maybe a swim might do you good. We're headed for Italy. We just came in here to pick up a friend. So, please just relax and have no fear. There is a storm brewing, but won't amount to much. We've double beam stabilizers and auto-balance pods for a smooth and safe ride."

"But, I have to catch Claudia up," Kaye cried in feigned distress.

"Is that your girlfriend with the huge 'north-and-south'?" he replied in a mock cockney accent.

"Rhyming slang?" she gasped, remembering Claudia's sensitivity about the size of her mouth and male vulgar associations.

"Nonsense, she'll be fine," he laughed and in that moment, Kaye sensed a man who loved comedy.

"What do I call you?" she shouted.

"Just, Mike."

Waking from her nap to answer an annoying rapping on the cabin door, Kaye felt the ship's motion, and kneeling up on her bed to look through a porthole, she could see the sun setting over a dark-blue, rippling sea. As she did so, a maid entered with a trolley, clean towels and fresh bed linen. A light was blinking on a bedside phone and there was a message, "Sorry, I've flown to London. We have a heliport on the top deck. Be back tomorrow afternoon in Naples. There's an infinite supply of drinks and a supply of good red and whites from around the world in your cabin. Enjoy. Mike."

Kaye laid back and thought about a glass of white -- "Oh gawd, I left that bottle of white in the freezer on Thursday evening."

This was not a new experience for her.

"Was it a screw cap or cork?"

She had damaged freezers in the past with both types of stoppers. By and large, the screw cap is the more dangerous, but only after the bottle is left in a horizontal position below -10 C for more than forty eight hours. Kaye had set the control knob at 'higher'. She was never quite sure whether that meant a 'higher' temperature or a 'higher' cooling power.

Imagining the stopper flying through the back of the freezer, propelled by the pressure of ice, she decided that only a glass of wine would quell her fears. As she was staring at the two glass fronted fridges, the phone rang asking if she needed room service or would like a 'table for one' on the star deck.

There are few pleasures which match a Mediterranean summer's, starlit night eating shrimp seasoned with a garlic and pepper sauce and drinking cold white wine.

Pausing, as we all do in those moments of extreme pleasure, she wondered, "What's happened to me?"

As the wines flowed and dishes came and went she wondered if she was being tempted by the Universe. Nodding her head, she thought it highly possible and decided to acquiesce.

The morning view from her porthole was of a coastline, and her breakfast steward told her, "Sicily ma'am. We'll be off Palermo at lunchtime if you fancy going ashore in the launch. But not enough time to see much of the place and its history. Naples tonight."

13: Sophia

Naples was reached in late-afternoon, and Kaye's knight arrived on board in a helicopter which then slid off across a sky that was slowly darkening in the East. As he did so, a short woman with stubby legs was helped out of a nearby barge. She immediately yelled to Mike as he came on deck, "Look *you*, we've got to talk. I've been bloody chasing you for five years or more. What's going on?"

The ship was rolling against its anchors and the woman's progress along the deck was very slow. One of the sailors, who was helping load supplies, gestured to Mike that he could carry her, but this was dismissed with the slightest wave of Mike's hand.

"Who the hell do you think you are?" the short woman called to Mike, who was watching her advance by pulling herself along the ship's rails. Finally, he removed his straw hat and smiled, "*Sophia,* so nice to see you. Must be what, five years?"

She stopped and puffed, and they stood ten feet apart.

"Okay, let's get you below decks, Sof," and he finally nodded to the same sailor who now carried her down a stairway, saying, "I'm Johnnie Walker, by the way. Not my real name of course, but that's what they do call me. Been on this ship for twenty years. Seen a few owners in my time, and now we got this bloke. Nice enough fellow he be. How 'bout you Miss?"

A steward came to the booth where Johnnie had set her down and asked if he could bring drinks. She asked for cold cider, adding, "It gets so hot in the Med this time of year. Oh please, could I have a straw?"

Johnnie repeated the words of a long-ago song, "The prettiest girl I ever saw was sippin' cider through a straw. Tell truth, I were born in an apple orchard in Somerset. Place called Saunders Bonk."

After some laughter, Sophia finally, replied to Johnnie's question, "I was Heron's first girlfriend, you know. Met him when I was selling ice creams at the Windmill Theatre in London, and I think gave him his first lay. He was pretty innocent in those days."

"That must have been a year or two ago."

"Twenty years. I was so in love. Still am. He's like a bloody drug. Once he pays attention to you, you're hooked. Used to talk into my ear, as he screwed me. Oh, boy. My skin would turn to goose bumps just thinking about him. Look, look," she pulled up her sleeve, "It's doing it now."

"It's just the cider, love, surely" exclaimed Johnnie in wide-eyed amazement.

"No, it's *not*. Same thing happens every time I get anywhere near *him*."

The steward looked up to see Mike standing at the top of the stairs and miming to keep filling her glass, which he did.

"So, in the end, Johnnie, I had to run from him. Seeing me and about ten other girls, he were, at the same time. We were all like a lot of mutts. Just sat there waiting for our turn to come round. So, when I'd had enough, I found an ordinary bloke to marry. Nice short bloke like me."

"So, it was all over?"

Sophia got herself comfortable across the corner of the booth, "Not quite. I was up in London with Tony, that's my hubby, and we sees that they're recording one of his shows in the Leicester Square Odeon and there are free tickets left. It were very good that show. I got backstage after it was over by saying I was an old flame, and he sees me."

"He remembered you?"

"Not half. Remembered me, alright. Locks his dressing room door and gives me one on his dressing table. Then turns me over and does the other side."

"Strewth."

"Why the surprise, Johnnie?"

"On the dressing table? How tall are you?"

"I'm okay from the waist up but I've got these confounded short legs. I was four foot ten and a *quarter*. And believe me, that quarter was important."

"You say, *was*."

"Yes, I've shrunk, you know. I think we all shrink with age."

"That's true, Sophia. *Shrinkage* is a serious problem as we age. I got a mate Terry. Works on one of them big cruise ships. Head steward, he is. Well, Terry has suffered a bad case of shrinkage. Down *south*. You know what I mean."

"Yep, my Tony's got the same problem. D'you think it's due to taking yer showers too hot? You know, like when you do yer laundry in too hot water?"

"Anyway, Sophia, you were saying about seeing Mike again after his show."

"I come out of his dressing room and looked for Tony, but he'd left word with the stage door keeper that he'd gone on back to our hotel. I was so sore down south that I could hardly walk, so I got a cab."

"Well, having a screw with Mike again, after all those years, was a nice little trip down memory lane for you."

"Well, as it turns out, it were more than that, Johnnie. I had twins nine months to the day."

"Does Tony know?"

"Know what?"

"Bout Mike giving you one. That is giving you two, as it were? Are they, I mean, *were they*, identical?"

"No. The second one took longer on account of his needing to find the – inner energy. Know what I mean?"

Most men respond to women talking about sex by a certain firmness of the loins. So Johnnie laughed and diverted his gaze from her to the stairs, and in so doing, noticed that Mike was gone, "What's your gripe with Mike now," he asked. "He didn't look that pleased to see you."

"Well," she continued, "I'm national secretary of the Women of the World's League Against Sex and – sorry, forget the rest. Anyway, *WOW-LASSIE*, they call us. We're like the suffragettes who fought for women's right to vote. Can you believe it was not until 1920, or something, that women got the vote? We were just like slaves with no rights. Now, we're making up for lost time. Fighting about the way men demean women by using them as sex objects. Just like cows in the animal markets."

"That's true."

"Johnnie, I have a very good friend. A girl I met through WOW-LASSIE. She's a leader in her field of nursing research. Has a job in the School of Nursing at Oxenbridge University."

"Where?"

"Oh, it's one of these old technical colleges that's found a spare bit of land in the London suburbs and changed its name. You know, all the old staff, most of whom are a lot of wankers, suddenly calling themselves *Professor* this and *Professor* that. Oh, thanks, Johnnie, yes, I'll have a re-fill. Very good cider, this. Not too sweet. Thanks, yes, this straw is a bit droopy. Reminds me of Tony when we come back from the pub and he's got lots of ambition in bed, but ability is *hard* to come by if yer follows me."

"So you were saying about this girl in the Nursing Department."

"Yes, now she *is good*. New staff, you know."

"Oxenbridge? Isn't that the place where the Head of Geography threw his wife out the window?"

"Well, *he* claims she jumped."

After an embarrassing silence, Johnnie continued, "You were saying about this woman in the Nursing Department?"

"Yes, right, well as soon as they got to be a university, they changed the Nurses Training Course into a proper Department. Quite right, says I. And they bring in this girl, Jennie Roberts, to be its Head. Before that she was a research fellow at Birmingham Uni. Her problem was that she was a lot smarter than any man, but looks like some Hollywood, Movie Queen. Well, now's her chance. So she gives this big speech at a conference on Medical Care in Modern Hospitals, and in the evening these cheeky, bloody, male doctors organizes a *Nurses Beauty Contest*. Can you bloody believe that? So all the nurses go to Jennie and complain that it's an insult to their profession."

"So Jennie calls the whole thing off?"

"Not a bit of it. She tells them to give the doctors hell and to all turn up topless."

"You're kidding?"

"No, I'm dead serious. Yes, thanks, just one more and I'd better be going. Tony and me are booked on an excursion tomorrow. See all the countryside round Naples and slap up lunch at some country inn or *ristorante* as they call it."

"Sounds wonderful."

"So, Johnnie, this Jennie's got the biggest honkers you ever saw and wins outright and tells the men that the Y chromosome will eventually die out as just a stage in human evolution."

Johnnie's hands involuntarily shot to his crouch as Sophia continued, "Apparently they can get two female eggs to combine to form a perfect woman."

Johnnie noticed that Mike had reappeared at the top of the staircase and was gesturing to him with that well known throat cutting motion of the side of the right hand.

"So," Johnnie continued, "I heard that Mike was in trouble with you girls for a bit too much tit and arse in his shows. Oh, whoops, sorry lassie, no offense."

"That's okay. Johnnie, I'd better try to move. Is there a ladies room handy? Wow, is it *me* or is this ship rocking on its anchor. Must be the sea breeze coming in."

"I heard, Sophia, that there's a court case in the offing against Mike. This *WOW-LASSIE* crowd of yours say they're going to take him to the cleaners and get his TV show closed down."

"We have the best women lawyers in the country, Johnnie. What Mike Heron is doing is blatantly against the Sex Discrimination Act. The secretary of WOW-LASSIE is a bloody brainy girl, name of Kaye something."

"That wouldn't be Kaye Fortie by any chance?" asked Johnnie.

"That's her. D'you *know her*?"

More desperate gestures from Mike at the top of the stairs.

"Okay, let's help you find the toilet," Johnnie reassured her as he reached out his arms to help her stand.

The ship was now meeting some heavy winds coming across the Tyrrhenian Sea. Sophia let Johnnie pull her up out of the booth, and was saying, "Men have got to learn to respect women."

At that moment, the ship hit a monster wave and Sophia lost her balance, and rolled like an inflated ball across the floor and out a long glass door marked 'WC portal'. It was actually a loading portal for the yacht; it was named 'Wandering Cloud' by Mike in memory of Mr Oliver's favourite piece of Wordsworth.

"Oh shit," Johnnie cried and dashing out on deck, saw Sophia fished out of the sea by the blue-striped sailors on the launch.

Opening her eyes and draining water from her mouth, "That's sobered me right up. Total immersion in the Med is good for the soul."

The captain of the launch asked which part of Naples he should drop her and she fished her room key out of her wet pocket to show him.

Flustered, he responded, "I'd better take you to the main port," and then in a voice drowned out by the waves, hitting the boat. "I assume you have your passport."

"Can you radio Tony to tell him I decided to go for a dip and for him not to worry?" This was also lost in the noise of the waves.

Then she called up to Mike, who was standing on deck, "You sod, I'll get you for this. Bastard. I thought that luggage shoot was the door to the toilet."

Mike heard nothing.

Then to herself, she muttered, "Oh bugger, here come those goose bumps, how does he do it?"

Mike called down through a megaphone, "Sorry what was that?"

Sophia squirmed and yelled, "*Bastard*. See you in court. That's the last of your lavatory humour."

The spray coming over the bow of the launch was soaking her, and the captain suggested that she wear one of the oilskins in the locker beneath the wheel.

Sophia, was in danger of not being able to re-enter Naples. It was late when she arrived and she felt wet, totally bedraggled and in a terrible post-alcoholic state produced by too much cider often secretly laced by Johnnie with vodka.

A bedraggled customs official looked down his croaked roman nose and smirked, "So you say your papers are here in Naples where you were on a tour bus, my child? Sorry. You need a passport to enter Italy."

With a deep, garlic yawn, which exposed his gold fillings, he continued, "Sisters of Santa Maria, can give you a blanket for the night in that shack over there."

A second officer woke from his slumbers with little nicety and scratched his genitals.

Rage growing, she shouted, "Look you Itie bloody imbecile, if I can't get into Naples, how the hell am I to get my passport? Just tell me that."

Italian custom officials have few skills in English, but their command of that language vanishes when there is a difficult question to answer. So, they stared at one another with all the facial and body expressions that have populated Italian Opera for the last few hundred years. Sophia stood waiting for an answer, almost expecting them to break out into song.

Faced with insoluble problems, Italians prefer to do nothing. So Sophia simply walked to the far corner of the customs shed and then into the ladies room through which she exited to the street and got a taxi.

Her husband Tony was a shortish fellow who hailed from Birmingham and was a supporter of the Aston Villa Soccer team, so he had learnt not to expect much in life. With their two sons, he was sitting in front of the TV in the Naples 'Jardinière Paradisimo' watching soccer, and turned to Sophia saying casually in his distinct accent, "Can't believe 'ow early in the year the soccer season starts these days."

"Mummy," clambered little Gilbert, "Daddy was watching a show on TV all day called --."

"-- Okay Gillie, let's go and make yer mum a nice cup a tea. She looks a bit wet and bedraggled, like."

"-- And Mum, there were girls with naked --."

"-- Anyway, love, continued Tony, what 'appened, like? I were a *bit* worried."

"Long story, my darling. Is there any of the duty-free whiskey left?

14: Audrey

Leaving Kaye, Claudia and Sophia on their various journeys, we must now turn our attention to yet another girl. She is called Audrey and, along with her, we will meet her University professor named Judith Cooper with whom she is destined to come to London to study. In so doing Audrey is destined to meet that long ago lost cousin of Mike called Denham who we heard about in our first chapter. We can reveal that Denham, or Denny as he known, is destined to make a very big splash and then disappear. But, never fear, he will be back.

So let us start. Audrey Smith was Irish, or at least the child of Irish immigrants to Australia. She had grown up in the tough, working-class, industrial suburbs of Western Sydney where her father had managed a grocery shop that eventually became a corner convenience store. As a baby, Audrey got herself caught under a moving car and, although she was rescued unharmed, the shock made her very wary of venturing beyond the house. So, she developed into a child obsessed with reading, which included every publication on her father's magazine rack, ranging from National Geographic to Playboy. She outshone all other children at school and was treated badly by the boys, especially during her body's transition from girl to woman. One afternoon on her way home, six boys ambushed Audrey and tried to rape her. Her screams were heard by two middle-aged women, euphemistically known as sisters, who came to her rescue. They then took her home for tea and cakes, always, and quite rightfully, considered by the British peoples as the universal panacea.

The women were both artistic and loved to read and paint. Audrey was invited to use their colossal library at her will. It was the start of a life-long friendship that opened Audrey's eyes to the world of literature and art. She went to the Potters University of East Sydney where she met Judith Cooper, the Professor of Literature and after three years moved with Judith to the Royal Sunbury College, London University, where she became her graduate student.

Most university departments have post-doctoral fellows and research fellows, who are not teaching staff, but spend their days doing research. In a sense they are perpetual students who never leave the academic environment and become founts of knowledge. They are guests at every Saturday evening party and take students out to lunch and spout their wisdom. And so, on her arrival at Royal Sunbury, Audrey was swept along to the Royal Oak pub by the very suave Denny, whose family name seemed to have been lost in the antiquity of the department.

"Audrey, I recommend the pie and chips. The bitter is good here and *cheap*. Let me tell you that my granddad was a Shakespeare nut. My cousin, Mike Heron, went on to translate most of the bawdier bits of Shakespeare into comedy, as you know."

"No, I don't *know*. Who is this Mike Heron?"

"He does a show on BritishTV. Very funny. Actually, I've never met him. My Mum thought that his parents were too beneath us socially, so there was a great divide down the middle of the family. Happens a lot with British families. They never associate and end up hating one another."

"So Denny, is this Mike Heron bloke famous or what?"

"Audrey, I love your Australian forthrightness. I would say that he very famous. But I'm not sure if he actually writes the show now. Or is even *one* of the writers. Or, none of them. Perhaps he's even *dead*." Denny laughed that laugh of the English intelligencer which was lost on Audrey.

Professor Judith Cooper invited Audrey and Denny to have dinner one Friday evening at her apartment, 8C Pemberton Road, in a district of London called Denham Groves.

The dinner was superb, and around 11 pm Judith turned on her TV, commenting, "I doubt this show has arrived in Australia yet." She was wrong BritishTV had sold the show worldwide and estimated it had a weekly audience of over three hundred million. It had turned Frank Kent, the owner and Director of BritishTV, into a millionaire many times over. There was a plaque on the wall of Frank's office with the words, 'If Mike Heron didn't exist we would have had to invent him."

It was a funny show. Few men or women could resist the simple humour. Mike Heron had become a modern-day Charlie Chaplin, with the combined genius of the great screen comedians of the 20th century.

11 pm on Friday evenings was now earmarked by hospitals as the peak time for admission of heart attack victims.

Denny rolled back and forth on the floor in laughter, and Audrey developed convulsions watching Mike's continuing change of costumes.

"On no," she screamed, "I can't breathe, Oh dear."

As the show finished, Judith turned to Audrey and with an Australian drawl, "What's so bloody clever is his ability to change from a smooth, gorgeous, bloody hunk in that beautiful suit and tie to an unshaven, little twerp in those scraggy clothes. Can't believe such a transformation is possible. The man's talented."

Denny was still in a paroxysm of laughter. Combined with a heavy dinner and a lot of beer, he needed to sit on the floor and then lay down and gradually developed a rolling motion back and forth across Judith's floor. His roll-path took him through an open French window outside of which was a balcony surrounded by wrought iron railings.

15: Pemberton Road

In Victorian and Edwardian times, the Denham Grove part of London was a fashionable district for wealthy families, and each residence had a dozen servants 'below stairs'. These stately mansions were now divided into comfortable apartments, and their rents would normally be expected to be too high for a professor of Judith's rank. But Judith was no ordinary professor. She came from the Cooper family of New South Wales who owned 'Cooper Graceman International Foods', a huge corporation that dominated the European and US markets in Australian cooked meats.

Her flat was once the private sitting room of the lady of the house, and the French windows, through which Denny had just rolled, would have been opened only on those rare summer days when the temperature in London crept up to what was then called 'mild'. But Judith had been raised in a country of vast open spaces, and she liked to feel the free winds about her. So, the old-fashioned fireplace poured out heat from an electric imitation log fire, with all the windows permanently open.

Furniture in Victorian London houses tended to be big and heavy, requiring large openings for its entry and egress, usually via upper storey windows, using a system of ropes and pulleys. Men positioned in the street below would pull downwards on ropes, and the piece of furniture would ascend to be finally grasped by men leaning out of a window, or, in the case of a balcony, leaning over the railings. For this reason, most railings around balconies had a gate which could be opened.

A good balcony must slope down away from the house. The reason is very evident to all those of us with a practical turn of mind and can be explained by the single word 'drainage'. We should also add that Victorian builders loved to cover outside steps and balconies with highly polished ceramic tiles. All of us who have encountered wet potting soil on polished surfaces would have certainly advised shutting that gate from the balcony.

Pemberton Road, the street below Judith's apartment was once quiet and gentile, but now had very expensive-looking cars parked nose-to-bumper on both sides, with a myriad of signs affixed to posts driven into the edge of the roadway telling motorists whether they might leave their car at that spot, and, if so, for how long and at what cost.

Immediately below Judith's balcony was a tiny garden with a small pond surrounded by dwarf poplar trees and a little ornamental Bonsai tree planted in a small tank. Noteworthy, the tank had 'George Specimens' painted on its side.

Had Denny's head not been so filled with Mike Heron's humour, as he rolled onto the balcony in his worn old corduroys, he would have noticed that rolling had given way to sliding. Reaching for the railings around the balcony in an act of self-preservation he also noted that they were 'bowed' in the style fashionable in the 19th century and still seen around London's stately houses and parks. Interesting though he found this observation, it was of less concern to him than the existence of a gap in the railings through which his trajectory was destined to take him in less than a second.

Later that Friday evening, some good Australian red wines helped Judith and Audrey analyse the Mike Heron's Show.

"What exactly is *Vaudeville*, Judith? Is that what we were watching on TV? It's just a name to me."

Notice there was no use of the words, 'Professor Cooper' in this conversation despite her academic seniority. The reason is that Australians hate formality of any type. As proof we submit as evidence the fact that a recent Australian Prime Minister was simply called, 'Bob'.

"Well, Audrey," answered Judith, "I did some research because it's such a *weird* name. Basically, what the British call *music hall*, is a collection of individual acts ranging from stand-up comedians to dancing girls. Mike could have done that, but he's much more than a stand-up. But, as they say, at the end of the day, hmm, I made that rhyme just in time, a comic is only as good as his or her stand-up performance."

"Where does the name *Vaudeville* come from?"

"That name evolved as most words do, through the shortening of a description of something. In the 1400s, the town of Vire in Normandy became known as a rich source of popular drinking songs and ditties with barbed satire and topical humour. Eventually any such song was referred to as *un chanson du Vau de Vire*, or *a song of the valley of Vire*. The clipped form *vaudevire* was in common use by 1500."

"Okay, so what's *burlesque*?"

"It's defined as a theatrical entertainment of broad and earthy humour; consisting of comic skits and short turns. Sometimes not for *family viewing*."

"So, Mike is closer to burlesque than anything?" asked Audrey.

"I believe that there are several people in that show who are marketed as *Mike Heron*," replied Judith.

Many men have noticed a very slight tendency of women to want to talk to one another often at the expense of ignoring all external sounds and other influences such as desperate cries of help or the splash as a body falls into water from thirty feet.

"Incidentally, where is Denny? Did he go outside? Through that door onto your balcony?"

They looked and found nothing. Judith had been working on potted plants on the balcony that morning before work and left the gate open. Now she closed it with a cursory glance into the garden.

Denny was nowhere to be found. They searched everywhere, high and low, but by the following Tuesday, he had not been seen and so Judith went to the Denham Groves police station and reported his disappearance.

"It's a bloody funny thing this," Police Sergeant Porkessen put his chin into his right hand, "but it's generally a Tuesday when we get these reports of lost dogs and cats."

"Incidentally," replied Police Officer Knowles, "I was just reading In the *Denham Groves and District Chronicle* that a postman has gone missing *and with him* all of the income tax notices for this neighbourhood."

"Well that could be a good thing."

"Another bit here in the paper, saying that they're going to widen Pemberton Road. All those little front gardens are to be requisitioned by the government and will become part of the roadway."

Audrey and Judith set about finding Denny's family. The University office knew almost nothing about him, which they claimed was not their fault. Traditionally, English universities ran on an unspoken word of trust. Staff were appointed by a slight nod from the Professor who often signed salary checks personally, using a lump sum given him each year by the Vice Chancellor. So, they phoned around at Oxford University and found an old record of him but no other address. His College fees were paid by Mr Bertrand Bolster-Benedictine QC, of Doyle, Doyle, Benedictine and Whartfeckle, Barristers at Law, with Chambers at 7 Bellend Passage, off Fleet Street, London, EC4.

Audrey remembered Denny saying he was a cousin to Mike Heron. So she contacted BritishTV and had a reply saying that in view of the serious nature of Audrey's enquiry, Frank Kent, who was responsible for the Mike Heron Show had phoned Mike, who was aboard his yacht in the Mediterranean, and he had agreed to contact her on his return. When he did so, he invited her to visit him in at what he called, 'his retreat at Hells Peak, near St Fuller, Cornwall.'

16: Ralph Rankworth-Humphries

The pond below Judith's balcony had been created by Mr Ralph Rankworth-Humphries in the early days of the twentieth century and we need to revisit that time long ago to fully understand our story.

Ralph Rankworth-Humphries was then the Conservative Member of Parliament for West Wessex and also the parliamentary secretary to the Minister of State for the Cinque Ports, pronounced by the English as 'sink' ports, meaning the five harbours established by the conquering Normans.

The parliamentary work of Ralph Rankworth-Humphries was not arduous, not to say 'totally non-existent', and easily conducted from his London Club, 'The Athens', at 312 Royal Mall. Prime Ministers of the day knew how to contact him, although they never did, and life was fairly easy until his wife, Lady Wessex, decided that they needed a pond in the front garden.

Many women are very funny about their sudden need for a pond and men are apt to form small groups in very quiet corners discussing the issue and agreeing that they are only two types of women: those that have a pond and those that are going to need one soon.

Ralph Rankworth-Humphries was not one to stand about in these quiet corners with other men and so was quite taken aback by this ponding suggestion. But, knowing, like most married men, never to disagree with his wife, he rang the bell for Smithers, the butler, and immediately gave instructions for ponding to commence.

In Lady Wessex's case, the desire for a pond had been brought about by events that we shall discuss

123

later. But for the moment, we just note that Smithers was unsurprised by the request and merely nodded slightly in that obedient way that butlers have, and asked obsequiously, with head tilted to one side, "Just one minor detail, *sir*. How big and how deep would sir like the pond?"

At Eton School, Ralph Rankworth-Humphries had never been good at mathematics and was confused by numbers that he could not count on one hand. So he replied, "I should say about five by five."

"Would that be feet, sir?" replied Smithers.

"Damn it, man, how do I know?"

"Well, sir, you being in charge of the Cinque Ports, I thought it might be *fathoms*."

"What the hell are you talking about man, that front garden is hardly big enough for a dog to take a pee.

Smithers took a bus to Telmer St Joseph were he engaged a local well digger to come to Denham Groves and create a pond that was well over ten foot deep and a few feet square, and then asked Ralph Rankworth-Humphries whether he should stick in a few peripheral trees for reasons of safety."

"Might as well, whilst you're at it. Good idea Smithers," he pulled on his cigar feeling pleased with himself that the pond had been built and understanding the lack of advisability of anyone venturing into such a deep hole.

"By the way, Smithers, why d'you make it so damn deep? The well-diggers head disappeared far below the surface."

"Hum -- feet is quite normal, sir."

Ralph Rankworth-Humphries suddenly felt he was making a supreme fool of himself and had memories of a good caning at Eton.

"Oh, I see, Smithers, yes, quite right," he declared defensively.

"And the trees, sir. What sort of trees would you like, sir?"

"Oh well, nothing too big. In fact, something quite small. Something shoulder high to a dwarf. Damn it man, just get it done before her ladyship gets back from the country. Make sure she can see the damn pond from her balcony."

"Well sir, I will need to know what type of trees you have in mind, sir."

"The sort of thing that people plant in front gardens. What shall I say: something *popular*. Don't bother me man about such trivia, I'm going to me constituency."

Truth be told, Ralph Rankworth-Humphries had never been to West Wessex and had no real idea how he might get there if the need arose. His 'going to my constituency' was code for a week-long game of cards at his Club. He might, or might not, be interested to hear that his parliamentary constituency of West Wessex consisted entirely of Lady Wessex's country estate. It had 82 voters when founded by her father Sir Omegustus Bunsbury, who was then the equivalent of the present day Director of the Parliamentary Boundaries Commission.

West Wessex was Omegustus's insurance policy should there ever be a critical vote in parliament affecting his considerable personal fortune. In later life, he became so paranoid that he bought diamonds in

Amsterdam and had them sealed inside a stone statuette of himself.

Most large cities, including London, Paris, and New York overlay underground streams which once flowed happily across open fields and meadows, upon which the cities are now built. These rivers now run through buried pipes and culverts as can be attested by putting ear to ground and hearing rushing water beneath the streets of London. Many of the birds one hears in cities are singing songs which may be roughly translated as, "What the bloody hell happened to our river."

There are maps available which show the routes of these rivers. It is advisable to choose a quiet time of day for this ear-to-the-ground river spotting exercise, and also a street that is both clean and free from dogs in urgent need of urination.

The very keen underground river spotter can also visit any of London's parks on cold mornings, which conveniently occur at just about any time of year, and see steam issuing from strange concrete grills. These are rivers which engineers have forced underground and have become heated by ancient geological faults, within which hedonistic fish can bask in Mother Earth's natural heat.

Unbeknown to Ralph Rankworth-Humphries, the pond that Smithers built was deep enough to become a part of the River Telmer which once graced a rural area destined to become the Denham Groves district of London. During the Middle Ages, the Telmer was well known for its ephemeral flow patterns: during dry years it would disappear completely, and the river bed could be used by horse drawn carts. An engraving on the wall of St Joseph's Church in the village of Telmer St Joseph,

126

which is home to a tiny brook from which the River Telmer is claimed to rise, reads: 'Woe betide him that doth cart the River bed whilst rains come on St Swithun's day.'

The original architect of the Denham Groves district of London, Albert Bolster-Benedictine had buried the River Telmer in a culvert which was well below the surface of Pemberton Road.

Were it not for Lady Wessex's pond, the River Telmer would have flowed happily past the Rankworth-Humphries home for ever more. The pond was very attractive to local domestic animals and what is left of the original Denham Groves natural fauna.

A noticeable feature of the pond was that it seemed to emit a warm earthy mist and Lady Wessex was apt to remark on wet summer nights, "Ralph, where the hell is all this frog croaking coming from. Can't bloody sleep for the racket. Tell Smithers to have it silenced. *At once*."

17: Carole and Veronica

Before introducing Carole and Veronica, we need to say that in 1910, Ralph Rankworth-Humphries was found dead, trousers and underwear around his ankles, face-down in a foot of rainwater on the floor of a little-used, and locked, outside men's room at his Club. The facility was normally only unlocked during the annual garden party held in the Club's grounds. It was the cleaners who found him while investigating what the Club Secretary described as, 'a very obnoxious bloody smell coming from that lavatory'.

The cleaners found its roof to be leaking through a large hole which Police Chief Inspector Haines subsequently determined to have been made by the momentum of Ralph Rankworth-Humphries's trajectory after he went out the window on the sixth floor.

"Well, I suppose," opined the Inspector, "he were in a hurry to *go* and found all the lavatories on the sixth floor to be engaged."

The Club Secretary sat with his jaw dangling in disbelief.

Puffing his briar pipe, the Inspector continued, "Alcohol gradually rots the brain," and, as he donned his deerstalker hat, added with Holmesian grace, "I'll alert Smithers to get him scraped up, and tell Lady Wessex to call together the twelve voters so that she can appoint a new member of parliament for West Wessex. There is a story going round that she has in mind the Bishop of Gostchester."

"Funny you should mention the Bishop," snorted the Club secretary, "he was in the Club as a guest the very last time that Ralph Rankworth-Humphries was seen here alive. I believe they played cards well into the night."

"You may have to repair these floor tiles," the Inspector used the toe of his shoe to tip Ralph Rankworth-Humphries upwards and saw, what most men know already, that near to death the male penis grows to a hardness sufficient to crack open a rock surface when flung at it with sufficient speed; for many men it is really the only thing left to look forward to after a certain age of advanced maturity.

Shortly after Ralph Rankworth-Humphries' unusual mode of departure from this Earth, Lady Wessex was told that war with 'these damn Germans', looked very imminent, "and although it should take us only a few months to give them a damn good walloping, it could be a bit nasty with a few million or so killed."

Her cousin's son was George Bates, the explorer, and so she summoned him to a meeting at 8 Pemberton Road.

George Bates was a burly young man and, in her opinion, was rather like his father before him, Alowishus Bates, also a geographer: in her ladyship's view neither father nor son had much in the way of intelligence. She remembered Georgie as a scruffy little boy always playing in the river at 'Sunningham', his father's home at Cayho-on-Thames. Each night the child had brought back a series of buckets of brown water wriggling with aquatic life which he called his 'specimens'. These were decanted into a row of earthenware pots in the kitchen, each notated with their date and place of collection.

His father tended to work into the small hours of the morning on his own plan to irrigate the Sahara Desert. This work produced a thirst that was best slaked with his own 'Sunningham Country Wines' which had been described by the Bowley District Weekly Review as, 'high in alcohol and unique in throat-wrenching rawness'. At 4 am on one such night, Alowishus had gone to the kitchen looking for a snack and suffered an untimely death through mistaking one of his son's specimens for the fish stew left over from dinner. Observing the corpse to have a strange reddish, almost luminescent, glow, George noted that the offending specimen had been collected near the drains from his father's vineyard.

Now sitting in the drawing room at Pemberton Road, Lady Wessex offered the adult George an annual stipend that would be paid into a bank account. In return, he would find a girl who would be prepared to marry him and together they were to take over 8 Pemberton Road as their London residence.

"Not saying that you can't continue with your jolly little boat trips down the Amazon dear boy, but make sure the wife is always here. All bills on the property will be paid by my lawyers. If anything *comes up*, contact them immediately. Incidentally, this arrangement lasts for five years. If by that time I have not contacted you through me lawyers, the house is yours. Bye the way, I may come back once, uninvited, to pick up a package of some personal items in a year or two. It's in a safe place outside and I will not need to disturb you in order to reclaim it."

Two days later, George was summoned to the offices of Brassworth, Brassworth, Wilson and Brassworth, Solicitors where he had a meeting with Sir James Riversworth-Stockingham who was the senior clerk.

"Mr Bates, everything should have been made clear by her ladyship. You're just to take charge of the house. No changes to the external structure or garden to be made, you understand. You are to write to this office every three months to assure us that you, or your wife, are occupants of the property. We will then deposit funds into an account to be set up at Grey's Bank, Little Dumpling Street, in the City of London for withdrawal whenever you relinquish the custodianship of 8 Pemberton Road. After five years Lady Wessex will resume occupancy. If she doesn't, the house is yours or that of your wife."

George was scheduled to depart in three days-time on a Royal Society expedition to the Amazon and therefore needed to work with some dispatch. Teaming up with his close friend the Hon Percy Warrington, they both found wives through an Introduction Agency, and both were married in a Registry Office in Chelsea on the morning of their departure.

Three years later, there was a rummage outside the front door of 8 Pemberton and there stood a metal tank, accompanied by a filthy looking George.

"Hello Carole, darling," he cried, looking distinctly happy. "I'm back. Need to find a place to put my specimens from the Amazon.

"Darling," she replied. "I was just thinking about you last year. Or was it the year before? Now don't tell me, you're just on the tip of my tongue."

George felt his three years of enforced separation from Carole coming to a lingual end.

"I've got it," screamed Carole, "you're Billie."

That was a terrible mistake, and incidentally the name of her baby cousin who was the first naked boy she had ever seen. The shock to her of her cousin's genitalia, which she mistook for an alien growth, was at the time so great that she cried to her mother, "What a blessing it's not on his face."

George patiently corrected her with, "My Dear, surely you remember. I'm your *Georgie*."

"Of course, *George* darling. Hardly recognized you. Seem to remember a much taller man. Have you shrunk? I mean, been near any of those horrid pygmies or anything."

"No, it's probably because I'm standing at the bottom of this 15 feet flight of steps and you're at the top. As I was saying, all my specimens are in this tank."

Specimens had been important to George ever since he was a child at Sunningham.

"Well please don't bring the nasty things into the house. Why not leave it down there in the front garden. Be safe as houses down there, darling."

So he did.

"Billie --," she added.

"You mean, George, dear."

"Darling, you're far too filthy for the house."

"Sorry darling, I've just left the boat. Amazon is a bit on the mucky side."

"If you go down those steps over there, you can open the door into the servants' quarters below," adding in her higher middle class lisp, "and wash yourself 'oft' with the bucket and hose that were kept for the dog."

Next morning, George was awakened from a deep sleep on the sofa, in what had once been Smithers quarters, by a banging on the upstairs front door. Just as Smithers had done a million times, George climbed the inside stairs and opened the great oak front door. Looking down the long flight of front steps, he recognized his old friend, the Hon Percy Warrington, who started cajoling him to join the Army.

"Be an absolute bang-on thrill, old boy, but we need to be quick else it's all going to be over in a month or two. Let's both go down to the Recruiting Office straight after luncheon, old boy. They've set up one in the Strand outside Weatherby's Chop and Ale Shop so that all the chaps can simply flop straight in."

On most days, Carole Bates spent her time in her sitting room. It was much more convenient for her than trying to keep up the whole house. The feudal days of maintaining a house full of servants were long gone: the War had taken them to fight and to fill jobs of national importance.

The Catholic canon law's definition of 'consummation of marriage' is:

'Spouses have performed between themselves in a human fashion a conjugal act which is suitable in itself for the procreation of offspring, to which marriage is ordered by its nature and by which the spouses become one flesh'.

George had gone off to the Amazon on the evening of his marriage to Carole and then off to the War on the day after his return. Carole had guarded her precious pre-marital penile virginity, and so, allowing for George's exhaustion on arriving home from South America, she was, technically, unmarried.

With the end of the War in November 1918, neither George nor Percy returned to England, and so their wives presumed them to be dead. By rights, the women should have gone to the Army Office to check, but that involved changing buses twice and then having to remember their husband's names. Carole, in particular, always thought of that strange man who had married her as 'Billie' and, although she knew that was wrong, she could not summon up his real name. Any modern-day psychologist worth his salt would of course explain that as a mental block induced by her phobia about men. Veronica, on the other hand, knew her husband's name but could not bring herself to say the word on account of its common use in Britain as a vulgarism for the male reproductive organ, as in, "Bout time we gave old Percy a bit of an outing when we get to bed tonight."

But one thing that Carole did need to take action over was the tank of specimens which was still on the front lawn just as it had been left in 1914. She knew that the Royal Society had funded George's expedition to the Amazon before the War and so she went to their offices in Carlton House Terrace, but they proffered the view there would be nothing left alive, or at least nothing of value.

As is often the case, the Royal Society was almost right, but not quite. George's aquatic sample had included several eggs which, during the warm summer of 1915, had slowly hatched into Piranha fish that had then used their unique dentition to become masters of the tank. More eggs were laid and became buried in the detritus from the Piranha's daily fish suppers. With the inclement wet years of 1916 to 1918, the tank slowly settled into cold-induced inertia, so typical of Britain.

After the unsuccessful visit to the Royal Society in early 1919, Carole and Veronica decided their best move was to push John's tank over on its side so that the water would drain into the pond and then fill the tank with earth and plant a tree. This they did, and decided to try their hands at bonsai. Carole wanted to prune the little tree into something which would be symbolic of the marriage she had been denied, and so Veronica showed her a picture in a medical dictionary of aroused, male genitalia and explained in detail how the apparatus worked.

18: No Dogs or Cats

A year or so later, Carole was about to take Veronica her breakfast in bed when she picked up a note that had been pushed through their letter box. It invited 'Carole and your sister Veronica' to a meeting of local residents to discuss the strange problem of the disappearance of all cats and dogs in the Denham Groves neighbourhood. Carole commented that there was always some local problem: when she had first moved into the house, neighbours had warned about the frogs. Now it was the disappearance of cats and dogs; well at least the frogs were gone.

For forty years, Carole and Veronica had been happy in Denham Groves with Veronica pursuing a successful career as a travel agent, while Carole kept house and accompanied her sister on the annual free trips overseas specially arranged for tourist operators.

Carole was sometimes left by herself in the house for two or three nights. For the first night, she was always fine and slept well, with no competition for the blankets. On the second night she would tend to wake every couple of hours and miss that soft little hand under the sheets. On the third night, she could think of nothing but sex and rolled restlessly around the bed determined to be good.

So it was when Veronica went on a trip to France in 1928. She left on the Sunday in pouring rain. On the Tuesday it was still raining hard all day and Carole, somehow sensing the rain had finally abated, got up at

1 am and made tea, which she took into the sitting room. It was a warm August night and she finally took her tea out onto the wet balcony. The stars looked so bright now the clouds had cleared. There was a half moon and suddenly she could sense movement in the garden. She hardly dared look, and assured herself that it was probably just local cats and dogs. But there was a dark, moving shadow below her. Screwing up her courage, Carole looked over the balcony rail. It was a person pulling up a rope from the pond. It looked like a woman with a black robe and hood. Then suddenly there was a splash and the rope and woman fell back into the pond.

Checking on the pond first thing next morning, there was no rope to be seen and Carole decided not to tell Veronica on her return. It was probably a bad dream.

The time eventually came for Veronica and Carole to retire, and, accordingly, they opted for one of their annual free trips to be to Somerset where they paid a deposit on a small cottage for sale at Saunders Bonk. It featured a huge apple orchard. Lady Wessex's solicitors had sent them papers years ago transferring them full title of the house and a local developer in Denham Groves, Mr Nobby Riversworth-Stockingham, was interested in buying them out at a price that would complete the purchase of their cottage and leave them financially secure.

For their final free trip, Carole and Veronica went to the Amazon region where Carole wanted to visit the village that Billie, sorry, George, had used as a base in his Royal Society expedition. They found the actual house where he and his team had stayed and the owner pointed to boxes that he had never collected.

"They've been here for all these years?" Carole looked in amazement.

"No, madame, since the end of their last trip three weeks ago. I think that Mr Percy Warrington was in charge of transport, but he must have forgotten. Mr Bates got a letter from London saying that his house on the Thames had finally sold. I think he had money at last and wanted a good time."

Carole Bates could almost hear her husband, what was his name, okay yes, it was Bill, no, no, it was John. John? Surely there was no John. Yes, George, that was it, talking to Percy at the end of the War.

"Perce, old boy, I'm heading back to the Amazon. Catch a boat from Amsterdam. No point in wasting time going to England. All that bloody rain. Why don't you come with me, old boy?"

"Don't you want to see your wife, whatever her name is? Carole that's it."

"No old boy. To be frank, I can't stand the bloody woman. Upper class bitch. Rather be with you."

"I agree actually." What's my wife called?"

"Bloody Valery, I think. Something like that. You didn't ever do you know what with her."

"Bloody hell, no."

Reader, between ourselves, he meant 'Veronica' but really four years is a long time and she had not thought once to write a tear-stained letter to his regiment. In fact nor had Carole to George, that is even if had remembered his name. Women tend to use men in much the same way as men exploit women.

So they went back to the Amazon, together.

They had been so close in the Trenches.

Fear brings humans together.

Makes lovers out of strangers.

Carole and Veronica left 8 Pemberton Road very much as it was, including the plants on the balcony which remained there through many tenants including Judith Cooper.

The disappearance of cats and dogs in the Denham Groves neighbourhood remained a cyclical problem. One astute long-term resident, Roselyn Harbury, who lived in 'Buxton Cottage' on the corner of Exmouth Drive and Pemberton Road, noticed that 'lost dog' and 'lost cat' notices seemed to be far more prevalent in wet summers. Since 1918, she had lost seven cats and five dogs; all during wet seasons.

Her husband, Alex, had also disappeared during the previous year. Search, as they might, the local police could not trace him. Taking their German Dachshund, Fritz, for his evening walk at about 7 pm one Friday evening, Alex needed to tie a long scarf under Fritz's stomach so as to hold it off the wet ground. The spectacle of Alex and Fritz walking the streets on wet evenings was a well-known comedy draw in Denham Groves: Fritz would run to sniff an interesting scent, and Alex would scamper after him trying hard to keep his balance.

Friday evening was somewhat of a weekly ritual in the Harbury household. After his walk, Fritz would be given a small dish of the Harbury's special Friday evening dinner and would then sleep until morning in his basket. This gave Roselyn and Alex some peace to watch TV, there being a few of their favourite shows airing on Friday, including Mike Heron at 11 pm. This always put Alex in the mood for what Roselyn called 'getting a bit friendly' in bed.

That particular Friday, Roselyn had prepared Fritz's favourite dish, lasagne. She ended up eating dinner alone; it seemed a pity to waste Fritz's portion, so she wrapped the leftovers in cling plastic and popped the package into the freezer. She had been looking forward to 'getting a bit friendly' and knew that Alex would have wanted her to take care of that matter herself.

On the following Tuesday, she posted 'lost dog' notices on all the local lampposts and dropped leaflets in her neighbours' doors. Then on the Wednesday, she went to the Denham Groves police station to report that Alex was missing.

For Roselyn, the really big problem was how long she should decently wait before thinking about having a new male buddy: Fritz had really stolen her heart and it was impossible to imagine that any other creature could come that close to her. She would often stare at that portion of lasagne still in the freezer, and think of his wet tongue and that long shaft of flesh, and decided it was time for a formal grave.

The portion of lasagne fitted nicely in a wooden box bought from the craft shop in the High Street, and they also agreed to engrave a little brass plate. Late one Friday evening, exactly a year to the date, she cursed Alex for not being available and dug the hole in the garden herself. A handy rock served as a little headstone and she painted on it, 'To my soul mate, rest in peace'. One last look at the little box, and, with eyes filled with tears, she did her little friendly playful bark and filled in the hole.

The following summer was very dry, and at last Roselyn succumbed to her maternal urges and bought from the pet shop a little wet bundle of puppies; there were two, based on the philosophy that she needed a backup. With the usual cycle of weather, the next summer was wet, and one Friday evening she had interrupted her walk to talk to Miss Pauline Perrington who was the new tenant of the ground floor flat, 8A Pemberton Road. The dogs set about investigating the dwarf poplar trees, and Roselyn allowed them to play by putting ten feet of slack on their leashes, knowing that they had already attended to their needs of nature.

She was quite distracted by the little bonsai tree, and, it being Friday evening, remembered that it was her night for 'getting a bit friendly', albeit unaccompanied. Only the smell of her dinner cooking slowly in the oven brought her back to the real world as she approached 'Buxton Cottage' and suddenly realised that her twin leashes were bereft of their canine loads.

Clifford J. Hearn

19: Smithers

We must now step back into history and discover how the butler 'Smithers' ever became the butler 'Smithers'. Remember he was butler to Lady Wessex's husband Ralph Rankworth-Humphries who was a Member of Parliament and also the parliamentary secretary to the Minister of State for the Cinque Ports. It was Ralph Rankworth-Humphries that had ordered the construction of the pond, about which we have heard so much. But it was Smithers who made it so deep. A pond 15 feet deep was really a bit excessive. Well, that is unless you have some ulterior motive.

But we must go even further back in time to meet a boy called Sam Larkin who had been trained by his father Patrick to break safes. The Larkin family had come to London, before Sam was born, in the 1800's from the Essex marshes to do what they did best: dig drainage ditches. The Larkins made enough money to buy a very pleasant piece of land in the country village of Telmer St Joseph called 'Smithers Farm'. Whoever this farmer Smithers was, is now lost in folklore.

By the time Sam was born, the demand for diggers of drains, trenches, and canals had declined, and his father Patrick then turned his hand to safe breaking in London. But he also had a thriving business as a *fence*, that is, a person who buys recently stolen valuables from criminals at ridiculously low prices and manages to hide them away for years or export them until they cease to be of interest to the police, or, in the criminal vernacular, they are then no longer *hot*. This business needed Patrick to return weekly to Smithers farm which had proven very valuable in hiding the precious goods that he fenced. When Patrick died, Sam sold the land which was eventually used to build a residential estate called 'Smithers Dell'.

Patrick had trained Sam to follow in his safe breaking footsteps and as they roamed London from one aristocratic house to another he passed the time by handing down to Sam the family knowledge of London's drains.

When the day came for Sam to burglar a house single-handed, Patrick gave him some final advice, "When dealing with the aristocracy, my son, always have a ready answer. Remember this, they don't know you from a bar of soap. To them aristocrats, all those what are not part of the aristocracy don't exist as *people*. It's true, son. We simple working folk are just serfs to them. We're only here to serve. So if one of 'em catches you at your work, just say: *I'm here mending your safe, me lord*. And give 'em a false name. Let's make yours – let's see – what'll it be? How about *Smithers* after our plot of land at home. Sounds suitable for a footman or butler."

"But what if I'm actually putting the bootie in me sack, Dad?"

"In that case son, you gotta think on the spot. Could try: *Just taking these jewels off to be cleaned, me lord. Very sorry to disturb. We're so overworked at this time of year. You know, Christmas and all that, we have to work at night.*"

"What if it's middle of summer?"

"Say, *what wiv all our staff on holiday*. Or, if it's the depth of February say, *wiv all this flu about*."

"Okay, I got it, but what if I'm just wandering the 'ouse looking for the bleeding safe?"

"In that case, just say: *Evening, me lord. Is there anything I can get for yer? How about a nice glass of whiskey?*"

So, on the night that Ralph Rankworth-Humphries apprehended Sam entering his study through an open window and exclaimed, "Who the bloody hell are you?" Sam had replied, "Just checking the security of this window, sir. One of the chamber maids reported hearing a strange rumbling here last night."

"Oh, I see, yes, certainly need to check any strange rumblings."

"Never can be too careful, me Lord. One day's strange rumbling is tomorrow's collapsed wall."

"Bugger me. That doesn't sound good. But let me ask you again, *who the hell are you?*"

"Your new footman, me lord. Just started this morning. So no livery yet. Can I get you something? A nice glass of whiskey perhaps?"

"Well yes, ummm --."

"Name is *Smithers*, sir. Oh dear me, sir, the whisky decanter seems to be empty. Shall I nip down to the butler's pantry and get a bottle?"

"Well, yes, good idea, but the blighter's probably got it locked. Goes abed at eleven, and so I'll probably be dead with thirst before he wakes in the morning."

"Leave it to me, sir, I knows a few tricks with locks."

So Sam had become a servant called *Smithers* and eventually a very wealthy one. There was no need to abandon his burglary career. Quite the contrary, in fact. Pemberton Road provided some rich pickings that he passed to his father to fence. After his father started a

20 year vacation at the Scrubs, he used Terry Quinsy, who operated from a garden shed in Camden Town. The money then went to an account at Grey's Bank, Little Dumpling Street in the City of London. Mr Jobling, the bank manager, was told that it was Ralph Rankworth-Humphries's winnings at cards, and Smithers would occasionally draw a few pounds from the account "so as to buy a little jewellery for her ladyship in my master's name."

Smithers was planning ahead and seemed especially well-suited to playing both ends against the middle.

Quickly rising up the hierarchy of domestic servants to become butler, he was a young and good looking man, with enough personal charisma to become both Ralph Rankworth-Humphries's and Lady Wessex's confidant.

Iris Bunsbury the Lady Wessex's mother had gone fatally out the window some years earlier after returning with her husband from a long trip to the United States, only to forget that, according to British convention, the first-floor French window of her bedroom at the Cliff Top Hotel at Beachy Head in East Sussex was not at ground level. The accident was exacerbated by the cliff top having been eroded by a recent storm, and the additional nuisance of a high spring tide.

Omegustus Bunsbury, the Lord Wessex, took the train down to Beachy Head next day and tragically reenacted his wife's death by going out the same window. They laid him and his wife to rest in Wessex Cathedral, and the Wessex Estate passed to his daughter the present Duchess of Wessex as the sole heir.

A few weeks later, Smithers was called into the Duchess of Wessex's sitting room on a 'matter of some delicacy'.

"Got a bit of a problem, Smithers. Can't find the family jewels. No idea where poppa stashed 'em. Thought you might help, you having a certain gracefulness of touch with things of value, so I do hear from the other servants. Be a reward for you."

"A reward for *me,* my lady?"

She smiled back and took the opportunity to straighten her hair so that her breasts moved very slightly with her raised arms.

So the Duchess of Wessex and her faithful slave went to Wessex. For Smithers this was a challenge and indeed a challenge of such magnitude that, had his father still had his liberty, he would have been called in to help.

Yet his help was available through Smithers visiting his place of residence. When he did so, he heard great truths such as, "always start from the floor up; people tend to hide things as low as possible, just human instinct to do that, son. Look under carpets and pull up floorboards first. Then search the bottom shelves of cupboards and work your way up. Take the doors off and pull 'em to pieces. Remove the pictures. Look for hollow walls by knocking on 'em with a walking stick. Get inside the fireplace and climb up the chimney. Then take the ceilings down. Do it floor-by-floor, always working upward. Then, the attic, and under the rafters. Next, the garden. Dig it up, leave no stone unturned. Then, the trees. Climb 'em and look for holes; look on all the branches. Then, the driveways. Dig 'em up. Finally, crawl down the drains. After that, drain the ponds and then the lakes."

Smithers asked his father whether he'd ever hidden anything.

"Course, son, if you're good at finding things, it stands to reason that you're good at hiding 'em. So the last place anybody would look is the best place to hide something."

On the third day of searching, Smithers found the statuette of Omegustus Bunsbury, the Duke of Wessex, watching him from a prime position on the front lawn in which were sealed diamonds bought by him many years earlier in Amsterdam.

"No reward for you Smithers, until you think of a way of hiding 'em at 8 Pemberton Road."

"My lady, how about me telling Ralph Rankworth-Humphries that you need a pond and a few ornamental trees in the garden at Pemberton Road. Make a good hiding place."

"You might be on to something, Smithers. I'll damn soon tell him. I'm sleepy now. Hunting for treasure is hard work. Bedtime I think."

20: New York

In July 1914, Duchess Wessex arrived in New York on the steamship RMS Mauretania. During the voyage, Smithers had reminded her of his reward for finding her father's jewels, and, on the last day at sea, Smithers and his silver tongue were allowed an afternoon in her bed. On arrival at the dock, she had some difficulty in walking and was still visually shaken.

"Smithers look after all me luggage and bring it on to the house. I'll go on and rest me tired back. Don't be long, because I am badly in need of a bath and cup of tea. I want me *Twinings* tea mind, none of this American muck."

"Yes, your ladyship and the exact address?"

"Good lord man, surely yer know it's the house at Norwich and 10th."

"But your ladyship, I think you'll find that house was sold by the master in 1902. You remember the little matter of the gambling debt at his Club."

"Absolute nonsense. Smithers, you are to leave my service at the end of this week. I will not be *instructed* by servants. I own you and can use you how I wish. That does not give you any rights. I shall give you no references. After you have delivered me to my house and made me tea, you are to recruit a replacement for yourself and then go and make a new life for yourself in America. *Understood*?"

"Yes, your ladyship."

Smithers, or *Sam Larkin* to use his real name, was like a man set free from a life of servitude. He could smell freedom. Most men who are suddenly set free fail to grasp the opportunity but prefer the familiar life of drudgery.

Not Sam Larkin.

After removing her ladyship's gold jewellery and pistol from her luggage, he watched her take it, and herself, to the house at Norwich and 10th. He had the vaguest of memories that his master had got a good price for the property in 1902 from a very discrete owner of a chain of brothels who was wanting to expand his businesses in New York.

"You'll find I've put you a diamond or two in your luggage, old girl, so you should be happy in New York for a good few years. We both know where we put the rest of the diamonds."

The Duchess of Wessex was indeed happy as she rode away in that carriage and little did she realise that she was just a tiny, tiny, bit pregnant.

Smithers walked down to the area of New York which housed numerous porn shops.

"I'll give you a hundred for the lot, sir," offered the pawnbroker.

"You mean a hundred ten dollar bills?" replied Sam.

"Oh, I see a comedian we have here. Look, if it were diamonds, my son, I could do a lot better. But this country is awash with gold from California. Not like the old country. There, gold brought a tidy sum. But here, no. They just use it for mending the roads."

Smithers laughed, "No, the diamonds are in a very safe place in London."

"Best I can do is two hundred dollars, my limey friend. Take it or get the hell out of my shop."

"Bet you don't even have a thousand dollars to your name," Smithers smirked and turned for the door.

The pawnbroker called him back with, "Okay I'll make it three. Seeing as you are a new arrival in America."

Holding Duchess Wessex's pistol, which he had removed from her luggage, he turned, removed all the dollars from the cash till, throw some gold artefacts at the pawnbroker, and then repeated the same performance in all the shops on the street.

Working as a steward, Smithers returned to England, again on RMS Mauretania, and after a morning at the offices of the River Thames Control Board, at Missbury Street in the Chelsea district of London, he took a train from Waterloo to Bowley-upon-Thames, bought a rusty bicycle and two hours later found a room at the White Eagle pub at Cayho-on-Thames registering himself as 'Mr Smithers'.

Next morning, he cut open one of the cartridges from Lady Wessex's pistol, swallowed a bit of cordite and then queued at the Cayho Army Recruiting Centre, only to be rejected as unfit, "Although," grunted the recruiting officer, "we may have to call on you later, Mr Smithers, if this war goes until Christmas. Oh, here's your medical exception card in case any of the ladies try putting a white feather in your button hole."

Fundamentally a thief, Smithers had been taught by his father to steal from the aristocracy; his role as a butler was merely a side-line. Left with a very substantial bank balance, a comfortable retirement was ensured. But he was not one to be idle, and a week later read an advertisement in the Bowley District Weekly Review for a partner in a fishing boat that caught eels and sold them in London's Billingsgate Market at five each morning.

As a lad, Sam Larkin, known to us as 'Smithers', grew to manhood on a diet of the cheapest food available, which was 'jelled eels', or cooked eels left to set in their own glutinous juices. They were delicious and eels were also traditionally served in the best of households as pies with mashed potatoes.

The live eels were at their best during wet summers when hundreds of tons of rich untreated sludge poured into the river from underground drains in North London. Smithers later experimented by adding his own choice of herbs and spices to eels to create 'Smithers Bitter Sweet Eel'. When he first tasted his recipe, he gave a Cheshire smile and, his memory of that Atlantic voyage forever vivid, "Tastes just the Duchess."

Within a few years Smithers, with his hair now grown long and grey, and his sickly butler's pallor burnt brown by the sun and rain, became an expert on the ways of the river. His butler's suit, collar and bow tie still hung in a cupboard as a reminder of his years of service but had been replaced by the scruffy attire of a boatman.

The years passed happily with Smithers leading a contented life. Single cheerful men are anathema to women; they feel this is an unnatural state of affairs and many of the local girls paid special attention to the looseness of their clothes as they swayed their bodies past Mr Smithers in the street, to which he responded with his still-remembered butler's bow: it was perhaps more of a discreet nod of the head with the eyes half closing in obedience.

21: Joanie

One sunny morning in 1934, there was a gravelly commotion outside Smither's front door, and a lady dressed in red with a big smile and even bigger hat called out, "Are you Smithers? I'm Joanie Rankworth-Humphries. Your daughter."

Smithers had been trained as a butler, and butlers don't react to news of any type no matter how unexpected or life shattering. So he nodded his special nod, "Good morning, ma'am. I trust your journey was not too uncomfortable. Please do come in out of the heat and perhaps I might be allowed to offer you a cold refreshing drink and *you might like to use the ladies boudoir, such as it is.* I regret that this is not exactly a house suited to a lady such as yourself, although I find it perfectly adequate for a humble servant such as myself."

"Can I stay with you, Dad, for a year or so?"

"Of course."

"By the way, I'm pregnant."

"Really, congratulations. How is your mother, the Duchess? Still living in New York or did she come back to England? Or remarry?"

Smithers had insisted the Duchess keep six of the dozens of diamonds from her father's collection before she hid the rest at the bottom of the pond. Those six would have kept her going for at least fifteen years but eventually she would have needed to find a new man to support her or gone back to England in the vain hope of finding the other diamonds.

"She just disappeared, dad. Took a voyage on a very cheap trans-Atlantic steamer and never came back. I never heard a word and assume she found some old wealthy lord who married her. Probably living in some huge castle somewhere."

Smithers looked around for a bigger house and found that 'Sunningham' was available being sold by George Bates the explorer. Half a year later, a girl was born during the wettest summer that London had seen for a decade. Smithers' partners on the eeling boat wanted to retire, and so he bought them out and hired a nanny for baby Skye so that Joanie could help him on the river. She was a natural, and very soon ran the boat and the morning trips to Billingsgate Fish Market while Smithers stayed home and taught his little granddaughter the wonders of make-believe game play.

By the time Skye was nine, she had learnt to dive for eels from the boat, and during the wet summer of 1944 brought home a sealed package that had apparently washed into the bottom of the river from a normally dried up creek. Smithers took one look and pronounced: "At last. Her Ladyship's diamonds."

This occurrence gives credence to the oft-used bit of advice: 'Good things come to those who wait'.

22: Wandering Cloud

We must now move forward in time and catch up with Mike Heron aboard his yacht who is just explaining to Kaye Fortie that Gozo, where they were headed, has been ruined by catering to the British Navy for a hundred and fifty years.

"It's just like school dinners in Britain. You know, what I'm saying, grey meat covered with congealed gravy and wet mashed potato slapped on top."

Mike was on her left as they looked to sea over the rail on the bow.

"I take it, Mike," Kaye replied, manoeuvring her shoulders so that he could not get his right arm around them, "you're not thinking of becoming head of the Gozo Tourist Board."

Kaye gazed at Mike in deep admiration, perhaps even love, but she was not prepared to forfeit her body which she saw as her greatest bait.

"Don't get me wrong," he continued, " it's a lovely island and they have some great fiesta's, with statues from churches carried on shoulders down tiny streets, accompanied by a vanguard of marching bands playing drums and trumpets. The communities have poured all their resources into the local churches for centuries. Gold everywhere."

"So close to North Africa and yet they're Christians," exclaimed Kaye, lifting Mike's right elbow off her left breast.

"Converted by St Paul, himself, my dear. He went around the Mediterranean being shipwrecked. It became almost an addiction for him."

"Hard to imagine with these placid waters," she replied starting at the mill-pond-surface of the sea.

Mike turned and rested his back against the rail, and, as he did so, he reached his left arm across her back so as to grasp the rail on her right.

His plan was to trap her but he was quickly made aware of its failure as Kaye slipped her left hand inside his open shirt and squeezed his left nipple hard between finger and thumb, saying, "I hear that men can be induced to express milk if a baby sucks their nipples for long enough. Apparently, quite the thing with the gay community in Amsterdam."

Twisting away, he cried, "But don't be deceived by the Med. In winter it's a savage beast. Come the first or second week in September all hell is let loose on the water. Try reading the stories of the Ancients."

"How long will you stay down here, Mike?"

"End of August, Kaye. After the Feast of St Mary on the 15th, I'll put this tub to bed for the winter, go back to London and start my winter's work."

"What do you do in London?"

"Lots of things including the introduction and finale for comedy shows on TV, you know. BritishTV."

"*Really*?" she exclaimed, still innocent of Mike's identity.

"Just good old-fashioned slapstick humour. You know, like burlesque or vaudeville. Ideal for Friday evenings."

"Must pay well."

156

'It's just that the shows give people what they want, and they're now shown all around the world."

"What's the formula?"

"I'd don't really know. I've always just done what I do. I'm a fan of Charlie Chaplin and even, believe it or not, of Shakespeare. England's literary treasure."

"But, pardon my saying, Mike, you don't seem funny. I would never have put you down as a comedian, and a wildly successful one at that."

"All comedians have to balance their personalities by escaping to another world where they don't need to be funny. I try to hold myself in balance by running around in this tub for four months in the summer."

"How long are you in London doing shows?"

"Rest of the time."

"What about Mrs Mike?"

"There's no Mrs. Need to be alone to do my work. Needs the whole of me, one hundred percent of the day *and night*. What's your job, Kaye?"

Suddenly Kaye felt the preverbal penny drop.

"BritishTV? Friday night? Mike, Surely that's the Mike Heron Show? It's utter boredom. Women are only good for sex and, what's that word, yes, *cheese-cake*."

"Nothing like that on my show, Kaye. Most of the actors are women and they design the clothes and do the choreography. Actually, in Shakespeare's own words, we are all just actors."

"RIB number two coming alongside, Mike," announced the public address. "Humpy coming aboard."

"You'll have to excuse me, Kaye. Humpy came out from London to talk about the TV show and had a quick hour's dive here. It's Humpy's greatest pleasure. Apparently born on an Eeling boat."

As he walked towards the stern, Kaye saw a scuba diver haul themselves up a ladder from one of Mike's rubber inflatable boats and then pulling off their mask walk to a lower deck, followed by Mike. Kaye tried to imagine him as part of the Mike Heron Show but it didn't seem to work, so she just admired the waves hitting the bow and passing along both beams. Looking up, she saw the person from the other side of the fence at the emigration queue, wearing the same, crumpled summer clothes and backpack, re-board the RIB, which, with a wave from Mike, headed off into the sunset.

As he re-joined Kaye, she asked, "Are you going to offer me a job?"

"What can you do, Kaye?"

"I suppose you need lots of tit and arse."

Mike smiled back. "I'm looking for a first class organiser, and I do see in you a lot of suppressed talent."

"How very condescending of you, kind sir."

"Sorry, I didn't mean it to sound like that."

"But you are the very important Mike Heron, and I'm just a poor secretarial slave."

"Kaye, let's meet in Teddington as soon as I get back and see if it works for you."

Drinks were being ordered. Kaye asked for a lemon drop, and Mike claimed his thirst had been waiting all day for a dirty martini. She sensed that she was going to have to work hard to stay as sober as needed.

"I think the essence of a dirty martini," slurped Mike is the temperature. This summer, I've trained this barman, but we'll never see him again. Same with all the auxiliary staff."

"Is the boat laid up for the winter or what?"

"Kaye, this year, it'll be at Monte Carlo, but it varies depending on where we've been and if any major maintenance is needed."

"Must cost the Earth to run."

"You're right Kaye, it does. Let's sell it now; could be your first job. I'll see you for a dance later, but we're now cabling up to the land phone lines and I have business to attend to for an hour or so."

This man seemed to have a lot of irons in the fire. "You don't have radio, or wireless phones, or whatever they're called?"

Mike gave a quick look around, then lowered his voice, "Not for my private calls. Too many people listening. Not until we get digital phones, that is. Just let the staff know if you need anything." He touched Kaye's shoulder as he turned to leave, "Do excuse me now."

Kaye watched him depart, thinking what an interesting man he was. Looking around she noticed lights on in a thousand boats anchored in the harbour, and music drifted out from hotels and restaurants. This was a world of which Kaye had only ever dreamt. She decided that she wanted to make the most of the evening as she went to her cabin to change. There was a rather slinky black cocktail dress she had bought two months previously to please Rick but never had the nerve to wear. There had been two almost identical dresses in the shop: one short and one long.

"You've got the figure for the full-length one, ma'am," the shop assistant smiled, detecting that Kaye was veering that way. Then Kaye pulled the skirt halfway up her calves upon which the assistant added, "And, of course, wonderful legs. I am so envious, ma'am. My husband loves a nice leg, but then, the full-length shows off the thighs and breasts."

"Sod this," thought Kaye. "It's like buying the Christmas turkey. It's no wonder that Englishmen call us *birds*."

And yet she knew that she wanted to be viewed as sexually desirable by men. This was an age when society had not yet accepted that we all live our lives on many planes; it did not yet accept that women at work were not on the same plane as women at play.

As she pulled out the long dress in her cabin, she prayed that she had not gained any weight.

Thankfully, she hadn't, and without bothering with underwear, it slid down her body in a cascade of black silk like water over the Niagara Falls.

"Wow," she uttered in amazement to the mirror, "I could fall for you babe. Look at that body."

Self-doubt immediately invaded her mind and she cried, "Oh sod it, these mirrors must be rigged. I need to get up on a chair."

Okay, put on the high heels.

That would add many inches.

"Wow, how did I have the nerve to buy these. Oh, yes, I remember, Bloody Rick and his crack about the follow-me-home and fuck-me shoes, back when everything about him was so desirable and all I wanted to do was please his masculine cravings."

"Why are these little buckles so sodding small. Men should be made to wear the buggers. Oh sod it, I've still got to put on my false nails. Let's see if I can stand up first. Whoops, shouldn't have had that drink with Mike. I'm falling forward. No, okay, must remember to lean backwards. Sod all men. Bastards. Especially Englishmen. Right. Now, if I can just step up onto the chair."

Clifford J. Hearn

23: Claudia Fortie

Time now to look in on Claudia, who reached Gozo and checked herself into the reserved hotel on Ramla Beach.

Gozo, like many Mediterranean Islands, was fighting a war with women who claimed the same right as men to have bare chests on the beach. There were little notices in the shops and hotels, 'Please just show us your smile'. Claudia knew that Kaye would be down there on Ramla Beach with naked chest if she ever arrived. In the meantime, Claudia enjoyed having a room to herself and now that Ryan had gone his own way, she could do some serious flirting without Kaye acting as her chaperone.

The room had a good view of the beach, but she saw only families sweltering beneath umbrellas in the dry heat. The sun was burning hot, and the feeble air-conditioning in her room barely made a difference. There had been one reasonably slim boy, with his dog at his side, on Monday and his very tight swimming briefs had worried her.

Otherwise, she sat by the hotel's pool constantly fending off waiters wanting to bring her drinks. When she did succumb, it was a thick glass full of ice shrouded beneath a miniature plastic umbrella, with half a juiceless lemon and a barely-detectable splash of liquor.

Dinner was a choice of dishes with individual, elaborate, mouth-watering descriptions on the menu. On her first night, she had chosen the 'Gozo Summer Delight' described as 'a melody of meats and salad especially suited to the warm Mediterranean nights and harking back to the Knights of St John. Enjoy with our matched wines from Gozo's distinctive vineyards, where grapes are harvested with love and in the words of the Gozitan author, 'brought to perfection by years of unbroken alcoholism'.

The waiter, who introduced himself as Paulo, brought her a plate of tough meat and a bottle of raw red wine and retreated hurriedly to the kitchen.

"This is not what I ordered," she yelled at his back, but there was no response.

Three glasses of red wine later, she noticed a lizard, who had joined her for dinner, gulping for air and then turn over slowly on its back and die. It was time for a safari to the kitchen, but a man washing the floor explained, "The Chef, he checkered out. Last bus for Victoria already left."

Victoria is the capital of Gozo, and after two further nights of ten-minute deliberation on the menu resulting in the same plate of inedible meat and a bottle of paint-stripper labelled, 'Premier Vintage Rouge', Claudia decided to take the four o'clock bus. It was filled with sand-coated children in wet bathers. By contrast were the old women with buns of white hair, and distant-focused dark eyes set in shrivelled faces, wearing loose, thick black dresses, and holding big baskets on their laps. The bus crawled along rough limestone roads, just managing to overtake sorrowful donkeys pulling wooden carts that appeared empty apart from a driver who sheltered beneath a dirty straw hat and always seemed asleep.

All around her was a dry, white and yellow landscape featuring strange hills with flat tops. Prickly-Pear Cacti lined the roadside with their flattened segments, called 'pads', covered in white dust. The bus stopped in towns built of closely-grouped limestone houses with narrow cool passages and huge churches. A woman climbed aboard with two chickens which she clasped upside down by their legs inside a sack. They sensed that their life expectancy was limited and every few minutes shook their wings with enough vigour for the sack to bang against neighbouring seats. No one paid any attention: women had been taking chickens to market since the days of the Phoenicians and probably using the same hessian sacks.

An open truck passed the bus heaped high with tomatoes for the canning factory in Victoria. There, they would be graded and the rejects sold in the open market at 5 am next morning. The cans would take the ferry to Malta and from there fly off to feed the world's ever-growing addiction to tomato-based meals. Workers at the factory were part of that addiction and happily considered that the cans that rolled so freely off the end of the production line were, by rights, their own. They took so many cans home that they felt free to exchange them with their neighbours and eventually canned tomatoes became a sort of illegal currency: women would arrive at the morning market with baskets of cans.

"I give one small can for two melons and that bunch of grapes."

"Are you kidding me, woman. One small can worth half that bunch and nothing else."

"Don't you adopt that tone with me Joey Fenwick, else we will see who paid his telephone bill last week with ten cans. I have a son at the telephone exchange who listens in on your filthy calls to that lady in Soho, London. I will tell the priest."

The name of her son was Rufus and he did have a very ruddy complexion, not through eating so many canned tomatoes, but through his love of the wild oleander bushes that were brought to Malta from the Greek Island of Rhodes by the Knights of the Order of St John. The flowers and leaves contain digitalis which is a killer.

"Take any two melons you like, my dear, and make sure they're big like your own," replied Joey. There followed the smelling, squeezing and shaking by which old Mediterranean women can detect the ripeness of a melon. It is an art handed down by centuries of experience and requires the wearing of a headscarf nipped lightly under the chin and a facial expression that warns onlookers of the wreath of the devil should they try to seal the secret.

Claudia's view through the window of the bus was a scene unchanged in tens of thousands of years. She saw Gozo in the dry summer season when farmers kept their sheep and cattle indoors. Had she waited another two months she would have seen the dusty landscape spring to life and the dry roads become rivers. Gozo has always been considered Malta's breadbasket, and the production of fruit and vegetables in summer has been enabled by deep wells replenished in winter.

A restaurant stood before her at the bus terminal. Its frontage would not have been out of place in the upper-end restaurant districts in London or New York, with polished oak details and bottle-glass windows, mounted on which was a menu that looked rather like the one at her hotel on Ramla Beach. A waiter appeared at the doorway in a floor-length white apron tied with a string around his waist above which was a black shirt.

Had she slid down a space-time warp? Her query was answered immediately.

"Sorry ma'am. No need to look at menu. Came with the shop front. Imported from factory in England."

"The restaurant is called La Shandra?"

"All the restaurants from the factory are called La Shandra."

"What food do you really have?"

"We're not open, but we do have cold beer."

"What type?" she asked expecting the familiar names of commercial beers which dominated the English market.

"Cisk Lager, and the Hopleaf Pale Ale."

"What's the difference between those beers?"
"Have different labels Miss."

It was Ryan who had taught her to be snobbish about beer. He loved to take Claudia off to what he called 'real' pubs, in very unlikely places, which only sold beer from 'boutique breweries'. They had paid very high prices to sit in very sterile rooms and nod knowingly at other customers as they sipped beers from stainless steel vats with strange frothy colours and names like, 'Californian Blonde' and 'Old Rustic'.

But Gozo was really only a peasant community in which beer was a strictly foreign import from northern climates; the best they could do was to make crude wines that were guaranteed to rot the gut.

"What time is the last bus to Ramla?" she asked.

"At three pm."

"It's gone? How do I get home?"

"Just rent a car. I'll call Laurie Tomas and ask him. Come and have a Cisk lager while you wait."

Two Cisks later, a small hairy man in a highly-coloured shirt, with an enormous gold wrist watch, emerged from a black Mercedes Benz and sat diminutively beside Claudia and, after slipping his wedding ring into his shirt pocket, asked, "Have you been to the new night club at Xlendi?" which he pronounced as *Shlindy.*

"No, well, what's the name of this night club?"

"It has no name. Just opened."

"I really just have to rent a car to get home," clambered Claudia becoming increasingly nervous.

"I bring car in morning," Laurie shrugged his shoulders. "What is your name, Miss?"

"Claudia Jones. No, sorry, it's Claudia Fortie."

She could sense a puddle of sweat on her stool and, looking across at a mirror, realised that her dress was totally transparent in the dying light from the setting sun. Had she really worn her black bra with this white dress? She was almost frightened to look down at her lap, fervently hoping that she hadn't worn that black lace G string that Kaye made her buy in Soho at Easter."

Laurie stood up smiling, "Miss, come on, I show you my cars. I have nice white one to suit your dress with the lovely soft black trimmings."

He put money on the bar and stood holding the restaurant door open, with lecherous eyes waiting to ogle her.

Their eyes met as eyes do meet when there is a sense of sexual adventure.

He was a swarthy man, probably the product of the Phoenicians, Arabs, and Europeans who had left their genes in this isolated little island over thousands of years.

"Laurie, if you can bring a car here, I will have a chance to cool off and then we can go clubbing. I will drop you off on my way home."

Claudia's father had served in the British Navy in World War Two and helped the fight of the Maltese people against the Germans and Italians.

"Mediterranean people will never give up," he had taught her, and as Laurie nodded to her now, she knew that despite her winning what we might call 'round one', he would not give up. A part of her didn't want him to give up, but she wouldn't let him win until her last night in Gozo on the basis that holiday romances must never be more than one night stands.

As she started on her third Cisk, she thought, "And where the hell is Kaye?"

24: Frank Kent

WOW-LASSIE were hard at work in Britain with their claims that the Mike Heron Show defamed women. The technique was to attack BritishTV, which aired the Show, by picketing stores that sold any of the products featured in their TV advertisements.

With heavy heart, Frank Kent, the executive director of BritishTV sat down to breakfast one morning, having been told yesterday that Gleeson-Randall, the biggest marketing company in Britain, would cancel all advertising contracts if the Mike Heron Show was allowed to continue that autumn.

Worse of all, only 24 hours were allowed him to make the announcement and remove all advanced promos. Added to this were a dozen writs from lawyers acting for WOW-LASSIE claiming the Show contravened the Sex Discrimination Act of the British Parliament. Failure to take immediate action would result in Frank's arrest.

The other directors of BritishTV had agreed that Frank was between a rock and a hard place, and so he had set up a meeting for that day to drop the axe. It was a heart-breaking decision because he prided himself that the Show had originally been his idea.

As a young man, Frank had been a comedian himself and then became a script writer for some of the big names in US television. In New York, he met his wife, Barbara Warren who wrote as the free-lance journalist, 'Bunny Warren', who at that time was doing articles on street theatre for the New York Times.

One evening, Bunny took Frank to meet Humpy and the troupe of clowns as they performed on a crowded sidewalk in Times Square. Over the next week, Frank and Humpy conceived the idea of what was to evolve into the Mike Heron Show.

"Humpy," he had asked, "know anyone famous that we could bring in as the front man?" as he and Bunny prepared to move back to England. "Also, know of anyone with money to finance it all?"

Humpy told Frank that all would be arranged. She knew that her grandmother's jewels had arrived in the river.

As Frank stared at his bowl of cornflakes, Bunny asked, "What time will you be back this evening, my darling one?"

Standing, he put an arm around her waist and replied with a kiss on the left cheek. This was a critical day in which he needed to settle the company's dispute with advertisers.

"Frank, dear, another coffee before you go?"

"No, sweetheart, I'm awash with caffeine already."

"If you have to let the Show go, how bad is it for BritishTV?"

"It makes us a lot of money from advertisers. But we've no choice. WOW-LASSIE has women blocking the doorways of shops that sell any product that we promote. And the movement is growing."

Walking with him to his yellow Jaguar sports car, she opened his driver's door. Smiling under his handlebar moustache, he raised his eyebrows, and with a twinkle in his eyes, reassured her, "Don't worry my little Bunny, it was good while it lasted. We'll just have to find a camel with a new Hump."

Frankentstein was the name used for Frank Kent by everybody at his TV Company. It was a name he loved, and encouraged for the sheer joy of its burlesque; he even had a personalized car number plate: *FKENSTEIN.*

Humpy was waiting in his office in ragged shorts and torn shirt and started to stand as he entered.

"Stay there Hump. How you been? *Where* have you been?"

"I'm knackered, Frank. But I'm more or less happy that we have the new series of Shows in the can. We should screen the rough cuts so you and the other directors can eyeball them soon. Maybe this week."

"Did you get away at all this summer?"

"As you know, Mike flew me out to Malta for a day's diving –."

"You're like a fish underwater, Hump."

"Yes, but no eels in the Med. We had an hour's general discussion about the skits we've been working on. That's when he came back to see you to insist that BritishTV stop advertising the Show as what he calls a 'tit and arse piece of porn'."

"Okay, yes, and I promised him that this autumn's Show would tone down all that 'cheese cake'."

"Mike was unhappy when he came back and wants us all to sit down together and think about next year. In the mean time we have to finalise this coming season."

"Hump, I need to talk immediately -- ."

But Humpy's voice was in full stream.

"-- Frank, we've been hard at it for months. We should all try and get out on the river together one weekend. Like the old days. I'll talk to Mother about a good weekend for it."

Frank shifted awkwardly in his chair and then went to the drinks cupboard and brought back bottled water.

"Or would you perhaps prefer a beer, Hump?"

"-- Frank, how about Thursday for the previews of the rough cuts. I'll need to work like stink, but I should be ready. We need to do that if the first Show goes to air in October. All the girls will be there and you know the way they like to scrutinize everything. One hair out of place and they make me reshoot. Can you check everybody's schedules? I had better move."

Frank sat and looked at Humpy. The Mike Heron Show was her life. Many people devote their lives to one project. That is the way that great works of literature, art, science, and philosophy are born. Working twenty four hours a day, seven days a week, they punish their own minds and bodies and destroy families and friends. Humpy had done that for the last years with one simple objective: the ever-growing popularity of the Mike Heron Show.

Humpy had loved Mike from the moment that she, as Skye, had first seen him at the Theatrical School of Wendsor County.

Frank assumed that Humpy was employed by Mike, who himself earned large amounts of money, but Humpy now lived alone in a tiny apartment in Teddington and seemingly spent very little money. There was no car. Taxis and trains provided Humpy's transport. There was a house cleaner, Mrs Lowe three days a week who had little to do because Humpy worked at Teddington Studios all day and much of the night. Like so many artists, she was committed to her work; her interest in material things was slight.

The pressure of tears was excruciating behind Frank's eyes and his face froze with tension."

"Frank?" she peered at him with alarm. "What is it?"

"Look Hump, before you go, I need to talk to you."

"Can't do it after I've gone, Frank," she quipped. But there was no smile or laughter. The atmosphere was heavy with fear as it is whenever people ask 'to talk'.

"What is it Frank? Don't tell me you need to increase the number of shows in a series. But don't worry, we can do it if you're really desperate. There's lots of good stuff that's not made the final cut which we could mix back in. Plus Mike can take longer slots to tell his traditional jokes. Have you heard the one about --."

She smiled as she spoke knowing full well that more Shows was not the problem.

Like must women she was capable of endless giving but to be told to stop was unbearable.

"No, Hump. Not quite," Frank drawled out the words. "Something --."

Fear in her heart as the blood started to pound.

He stared at the top of his desk.

Her mouth was dry and she tried to take a deep swallow of the bottled water but somehow it just ran down her cheeks.

"Am I too expensive?" she pretended to joke.

They sat staring at one another.

"Idiot. I pay you nothing and the costs of producing these Shows must have skyrocketed. Where does the money come from?"

Only we, reader, know about the Duchess's diamonds.

In that moment, Humpy guessed and accepted the truth within herself, but, outwardly, she continued to fight.

The woman in her smiled, "So, what is it Frank? Come on you look miserable. We can't have that. I can increase the 'tits and arse', but Mike will go through the bloody roof. We're too blatant already, in his view, and insists that everything be very subtle and rely on the imagination. He's bloody conservative. If we're not careful, he'll pull out completely."

The tension eased and Frank tried to think of a leading sentence to start his terrible news.

"Hump. It's this WOW-LASSIE crowd."

She tried to dismiss the whole WOW-LASSIE threat. Laughing without, any true belief, "Frank, surely, Mike took care of all that nonsense. There was a long session between him and Jennie Roberts last winter, and he had Kaye Fortie onboard Wandering Cloud. That was really a piece of luck for him. I spotted her at Malta Airport and he rushed like a knight in shiny armour to rescue her from the heat and dust to the comfort of this yacht."

Frank stood shaking his head.

"No, No, No. Humpy," he almost shouted. "Whatever Mike did or didn't do, the writs are coming in, and the advertising agents are pulling out at such a rate that this TV company is going to be broke in a few weeks. Probably days."

"Frank, please don't be depressed. Actually, there was that woman, Sophia Fletcher, from WOW-LASSIE harassing him while I was on the boat. That woman is bloody predatory, and he cannot get rid of her. I suspect she's a big mover and shaker in WOW-LASSIE.

What say I go and try to get her on our side? Maybe give her a chance to actually do something on the Show. Come in and play the part of a protestor or something. Could work. She has a great little body. Could be photogenic."

But Frank was silent and stared out the corner window at the parking area filled with cars including his own yellow Jaguar, bought as a reward to himself for his success.

The moments passed.

Silence.

Then, with a deep breath, "Hump, it's too late."

"Frank, what are you saying?"

"We are pulling out of our contract with you and Mike, effective immediately. A press release will be issued at midday."

Frank Kent showed his true character in the decision to dump Humpy in order to save his own neck.

Hit with life changing news most of us fail to realise its significance and continue with trivial issues.

"What will happen to Mike?"

"He's facing a dozen private writs in court next week. After that I suppose he will simply go back to *stand-up*."

"But Frank, let's remember that it was *you* that invented this show." She raised her voice for the first time.

"No, Hump, it was you that had the basic idea," he pared. "And a bloody good idea it was."

Continuing her growing annoyance, "And Frank, you insisted that we needed a big male comedian's name to launch it and give it that edge. A show to titillate the boys. Ever since his Windmill days, people associate Mike with things a little risqué. And that is what you bloody got."

But Frank was fundamentally a business man and seeing her anger starting to surface decided to humour her with, "Agreed. Humpy, it was you that wanted the show to feature Mike Heron. And again it was a bloody good idea."

Frank Kent was eager to praise Humpy provided he could not be accused of any creative responsibility for the Show.

Humpy turned to Frank with eyes filled with crocodile tears while she tried to think ahead of him.

"What shall *I* do?" she invited him to reveal his own plans.

"Take a long holiday, Hump. You certainly deserve it. I'll pick up all the newly recorded shows later today. Store them away for the future."

Humpy's mind was quickening and she was realising that the material prepared for that autumn's series was not yet Frank's property. It would only have been Frank's property after Mike had been paid a massive fee. And if the Show was discontinued immediately that would not happen. The way things were going, Frank aimed to continue to make money from all her hard work. She determined that was not going to happen.

Hump had to think quickly.

Yes, Tiny Tim was the answer.

It was a ten minute ride from Frank's office to pick up all the film and tapes from BritishTV Studios in Teddington. Once they were packed in cases Humpy got a taxi to Euston Station and boarded the night train for

Edinburgh, then changed for Inverness, and finally took the single track railway to Thurso in the county of Caithness in the far north east of Scotland. Then another taxi to McLeod Lodge on the banks of Loch Calder where Timothy Paul heaved the three suitcases to the west tower, provided a double tot of malt whiskey, pulled the bed covers over the sleeping body and turned off the light with the comment, "Lassie, you have no woe now. You'll wake you in a day or two."

Despite his outward trappings of Laird of the Glen, Tim Paul was a third generation American actor who had helped Humpy set up the Clown Troupe in New York. A tiny man, his diminutive height had made him the perfect crowd-pleaser as he rolled and somersaulted through their legs as 'Tiny Tim'.

After Humpy came back to London several years ago to start the Mike Heron Show, Tim decided to return to his family roots in the north of Scotland. Rotting away, McLeod Lodge had an old 'For Sale' sign waving in the wind. The estate agent, Jock McDonald, had come out to Loch Calder to meet Tim and a deal was done in five minutes for a sum equivalent to a week's rent in the upper west side of Manhattan. As Jock was leaving, Tim asked why the landscape was so bleak and devoid of trees or any sort of agriculture. Jock lent out of his car window and replied, "You canna farm Caithness," to which Tim retorted, "Why?" raising a laugh from Jock, "Tim, you'll soon see when the winter brings the winds."

25: Death on the Beach

As Humpy arrived in Scotland, Claudia was waiting for Laurie to arrive at La Shandra Restaurant in Gozo's capital city, 'Victoria', named by the English overlords, after the queen of that name, and also known as 'Rabat' by the Maltese. She was expecting a rental car, and, surprisingly, she actually got one. It was a white convertible made by Toyota many years ago.

"Very sorry, Miss, but not time yet to clean properly. Please bring to my garage tomorrow, but vacuum not working today because my brother go to Malta for new hose, you understand?"

The inside of the car looked so filthy with sand and debris that she knew that it would ruin her now-dry white dress. Laurie seemed to crumble as a man as he realised that the car was a disgrace to his image.

"What about that black Mercedes that you drove up in earlier?"

Laurie had changed his shirt and put his gold wedding ring back on his finger.

"Are you married?" she asked

"I no live with Mary. She very *good* woman. She no let her priest apply to Pope for special dispensation for end of marriage. So she live with the nuns in the convent."

"You live alone?" asked Claudia walking back into the restaurant and sitting back on her stool.

"Gracie, my secretary, is friend and maybe one day we marry."

Claudia felt that she had gone back to the Middle-Ages.

"The Pope? The priest? Convent?"

Claudia finally walked out to the rental car. Standing beside it, she took off her dress by pulling it upward over her head, and then folded it as a cushion beneath her as she climbed onto the driver's seat. Fortunately Malta has inherited the British convention of driving on the left side of the road.

Laurie was a man whose dreams suddenly came true, but, in that moment, he felt a great need to protect the child before him. Like all women, Claudia had a natural tendency to take command and smiled, "Let's go clubbing, Laurie. Come on, don't be shy." With his mouth still hanging open, he yanked on the passenger door and lent across and put his white shirt over her bare shoulders."

Most men like their first view of a girl's body to be exclusive to them, but already the men who had previously been sitting idly around the bus terminal were forming a human wave that was sweeping towards Claudia. With a flick of the keys, which were still in the ignition, Claudia drove towards the setting sun and arrived in the market square.

Every morning at 5 am, the market square was filled with market stalls selling all manner of foods brought in by farmers. But now, in early evening, it was empty: the stalls had gone and the square had been swept and washed clean. A slow trickle of men, women, and children dressed in black climbed the steps of the church at one end of the square. Buildings were squashed tight together around the square and some housed shops, all of which were now closed and boarded. Claudia had driven into the square through a tiny alleyway between these buildings. The square was deep in shadow but the only way out seemed to be an alleyway similar to that through which she had just entered and both had large signs in English, 'No Exit' to which Laurie commented, "Please don't worry, it just means *No Entry*."

There are some etymological problems which are best ignored when you are driving an ancient open-topped car, almost naked, through the capital of a strange Mediterranean Island with a strict Catholic morality code dating back to St Paul, and a dark, swarthy, very randy man virtually dripping with testosterone sitting close beside you, his fingers already exploring the waist strap of your G string.

An old lady ran out to them from the roadside with a black scarf which she put over Claudia's head, "Miss, you must cover your hair this evening, it's the feast of Saint Abebus."

"Laurie, there's something wrong with this car. It seems to lollop along rather than drive smoothly."

"Let me get out and look for you, Miss."

With Laurie's head bent down to look at the wheels, Claudia took the opportunity to get her G string to sit properly around all the hills and valleys of her lower body.

"Well that's better," she whispered to herself as he climbed back in the car and asked, "So, what's the problem?"

"They put too big wheel on front right side."

"You mean one of the wheels is too big?"

"Don't worry, Miss. It's good while we drive north because of the rotation of the Earth. I change it to other side when we drive back."

Claudia sat open-mouthed in amazement.

"I give you discount on first-day hire."

"Where did you hear this nonsense about the rotation of the Earth?"

"From girl in Melbourne, whose grandfather come from Florida. But Earth rotate the other way in Australia. That why hot in winter." He seemed very content with both explanations and eager to resume the journey.

"Okay, Laurie, let's just get me home to my hotel. I'm hungry, but I suppose it's paint stripper and boot leather again for dinner. Look, you'd better drive."

The ocean winds had picked up during the day and blown sand high up the road leading to Ramla Beach, so the car was on the beach well before Laurie had expected. At least that was his story to Claudia.

"Don't worry, Miss, I have it towed out in morning. Tow truck at garage."

"What about the tide? Oh, okay there are no tides in the Mediterranean. That's why Julius Caesar lost all his boats when he came to Britain."

Needing a toilet very soon, so that all that Cisk lager could find a new home, she was conscious that the car was rapidly sinking into the soft sand, making her anxious to remove herself with all due speed. So, with no further delay, she jumped up, grabbing her shoes and bag from the floor, and asked Laurie for her dress on which he was sitting. There was a moon overhead, and to Laurie's lovesick eyes it turned her into a beautiful apparition. Standing slightly, so as to be able to haul her dress from under him, he lost his balance, toppled sideways, and grabbed hold of her to steady himself. At that moment, the car slid forward in the sand and Laurie fell back into his driver's seat with Claudia's head in his lap.

"Okay," she thought, "I might as was well get this over with, here and now, so I can get back to the hotel."

He did not object.

Five minutes later she scrambled up to the bushes, made herself sick, passed the Cisk lager, redressed and, finding that the shower was inoperative at the hotel, plunged into the pool and was soon seated in the dining room. Her usual waiter Paulo came running to her excitedly, "Miss, I have news."

"First can you get me some bottled water, coke wine, anything."

"Yes, Miss but *first* my news."

"*No. First* bring me water."

Claudia wondered if Laurie had found his way to the hotel. She hoped not because she had nothing more for him. That was one of her 'Class A' blow jobs. Ryan had classified them, and they usually only indulged in a 'Class A' when things were particularly harmonious. It had left her tongue feeling like a rasp and she swallowed two glasses of the lukewarm Perrier water brought by Paulo.

"What sort of *news*, Paulo?"

He scrunched up his face, "I forget Miss."

"You seemed quite excited about it earlier."

In Gozo, information is precious, and she suspected that Paulo had realised that he now had a bargaining chip.

"Was it news for me? My name is Claudia Jones, no sorry, it's Claudia Fortie."

Of course she was single. That thought filled her with excitement, and she realised that Laurie had been her first male conquest. Or perhaps 'act of self defence' might be a more accurate term. She remembered the girls at college saying Mediterranean men tasted different.

"Oh, damn," she muttered to herself, "I forgot to notice. Come to think of it. Oh dear that was a bad pun. Yes, come to think of it, there was a slight taste of – not garlic – Malta is not a Latin country – but of Britishness -- what is it? --- fish and chips and Heinz Salad Dressing."

Ryan had always tasted of cabbage until that dreadful day that she detected another woman. Okay, don't go there, it's all over now.

Actually with Laurie, a sand fly, or rather a veritable horde of sand flies, had descended on the car at the crucial moment and several had been fighting with her mouth for possession of his manhood.

So, being single, she could use her femininity to her own advantage. Ryan had always praised her as being the very best. Needing to run urgently to the bushes, she had to push Laurie sideways to extract both her thumbs out from his g spot. Anyway, she felt sure he was okay.

"Your name is Claudia Jones?" Paulo confirmed. "Phone message from your sister, Miss. Please to call her back. She leave you ship phone number."

At that moment her sister Kaye was concerned about the fit of her black silk dress that she intended wearing for dinner with Mike aboard his yacht, The Wandering Cloud.

186

Kaye's phone rang. "Okay, it must be Claudia," she thought. As soon as the yacht had got into port two hours ago, the land lines had been connected.

"K darling are you *O K*."

"Claudia, I do wish you'd stop that stupid joke. You're been doing it for nearly thirty years. "

"*I wasn't* joking, I mean *where are you,* and what's going on?"

The Gozo ambulance had arrived at Ramla Beach and Claudia walked the hotel phone on its long cord over to the front door to get a better view of the beach.

"Claudia, is that an ambulance I hear? Are you alright? Darling, what the hell is going on in Gozo?"

"Think it might be this guy that I sort of dated this afternoon."

"Sort of dated?"

"Well we ended up in his car on the beach and I had to calm him down. You know. Not calm him down exactly, but more give him the relief he needed."

"Relief? Not sure what you mean. Oh no, you didn't blow him off?"

"I had no other choice."

There was silence.

"What do you mean, you had *no other choice*?"

Kaye was almost deafened by the siren coming down the phone.

"I needed to do it to protect myself. Actually, it's been a while for me too. I enjoyed it as well. Don't tell me, I'm a married woman because *I'm not.*"

"Claudia, you didn't give him a *Class A.*"

"So *what if I did*?"

"You used both your thumbs?"

"Of course, how else could I do a *Class A*?"

At that moment Paulo burst into the foyer of the hotel with news that he would be retelling for the rest of his life. Things like this just didn't happen on Ramla Beach.

The words tumbled out of his mouth in a torrent of jumbled excitement, "Man dead on beach in car. Police everywhere. Listen, there goes the ambulance."

"Claudia, I think you've killed the bugger."

26: Considering the Situation

By this time, Humpy was rested and, leaving all the tapes and film with Tim Paul, travelled south to Cayhoon-Thames. Joanie was aging but still ran the eel business which would often take her away on sales tours for many weeks. Mrs Cotton, the house keeper, tended to all Humpy's needs so that afternoons could be idled away dreaming in the winter sun and reminiscing comic skits and themes. Always there were images of Mike.

"The first thing about comedy is getting the audience to suspend belief," Humpy remembered Mike Heron telling the kids at the Theatrical School of Wendsor County during his annual invited celebrity lecture. "That's also true in drama, but the comedian must do it in only a tenth of a second."

Looking down at the rows of children with their smiling young faces, he continued, "If you know that the audience is going to be difficult, try an easy non-confrontational first joke."

A hand went up from the audience and he nodded to a fresh-faced girl.

"Sir, how do you mean *non-confrontational*?"

"I mean nothing that immediately confronts them with the need to suspend major belief. So, don't start with *A Bishop, a lawyer, and a doctor were marooned on a desert island*."

"I don't understand, sir," came a voice from the front row."

"Well," responded Mike, "is it really very likely that a bishop, a lawyer and a doctor would be marooned on a desert island?"

The headmaster and several of the staff were already in fits of laughter. Mike's timing was perfect. Everybody wanted the punchline.

Just listening to Mike was funny.

"Okay," he raised his voice slightly, "Let's have a quick, easy joke just to calm down. Why did the chicken walk across the road *softly*?"

He turned to the audience with his hands raised waiting for an answer.

Not a sound.

"Well," he raised his eyebrows, "because the poor chicken couldn't walk, *hardly*."

Listening to laughter is rather like watching one's lover come to orgasm. Perhaps it kindles a sense of power but, more importantly, it strengthens the intimate bond between lovers. As the laughter died away, he knew they needed one more.

"My best example of a joke that is non-confrontational is one that my father, Wally Heron, told me. It was his favourite joke. It is non-confrontational because it starts so innocently and you don't even think there is a joke. And then it hits you at the last moment."

Looking out over a sea of open-mouthed expectation, Mike wondered if the joke that he had in mind was too subtle. Close to breaking his own rule of never hesitating in front of an audience, he decided that he would try to make it work.

"Two men met in the entrance hall of a London hotel.

"Hello sir, "greeted the first man, "didn't I meet you at Monte Carlo last year."

The second man looked aghast, "No, I wasn't at Monte Carlo last year."

The first man looked at the second and laughed, "now come to think of it, neither was I."

Mike looked at his audience and was pleased to see the expected worried glances between their faces.

Timing was important.

"So," the first man continued, "must have been two other men."

The explosion of laughter.

He'd made it.

A nod of admiration from the headmaster in recognition of the most difficult of joke styles.

Humpy stretched out on the porch one morning and remembered Lionel Bart's song, 'Reviewing the Situation' from his musical 'Oliver' based on Charles Dickens's novel, 'Oliver Twist'. It was sung by the arch-villain Fagin to whom Mike had been likened by WOW-LASSIE. The Daily Express newspaper had a headline 'Mike Heron in Denham Groves Court,' which went on to detail a long list of charges against him. The article wrote that Mike had appeared briefly, and his lawyer had applied for an adjournment. One short woman had been arrested and charged with contempt for yelling out, "You bastard, we'll get you. Sodding user of women."

Humpy had plenty of material in hand. First there was all of that autumn and winter's material, already filmed, and left with Tiny Tim. Now three more notebooks full of new ideas for skits that she had written here in Cayho.

Smithers' life style of so many decades ago was evident in black and white photographs spread around 'Sunningham' with pictures of the London butler turned river bum.

A week later Joanie ran from her car waving a copy of the London Times with pictures of Mike going into court under the headline, 'Mike Heron versus the Fems.'

"Love these pictures of the two groups of protesters," screamed Humpy. "Wow, I have got to do this as a skit on the Show."

"Excuse me Hump, you don't have a show anymore. The Mike Heron Show is as dead as the Dodo."

"Will you please stop that, mother. We will do it all under a different name."

"You're right, my girl. Glad to see you're back in fighting mode. A week or two by the river can cure the most severe of malaises."

"Plus the wonderful things Mrs Cotton can do with eels."

"Talking of which, Skye, I just sold ten thousand cases to the Italians. Told them they are best washed down with good dark reds followed by grappa."

"That reminds me, mum. You need more gin."

"By the way Skye, how's the money from the diamonds holding out?"

The two groups of protesters in the newspaper photographs were basically *pro and contra* the Mike Heron Show. The contra group were supporting WOW-LASSIE and prosecuting Mike Heron for his illegal exploitation of women under the Sex Discrimination Act. The pro group had been hurriedly assembled by the girl production staff at the Teddington Studies and had borrowed the costumes used in the shows. These were fairly skimp, and the girls took the opportunity to entertain the several hundred press reporters that arrived with photographers. The crowd surrounded the Denham Groves Magistrate's Court and a bus load of prostitutes from London's Soho district, all wearing tee shirts emblazoned with, 'First One Free', had been shipped in by Frank Kent's TV company to satisfy what he called 'the seamy side' of viewers interest. The expected audience that evening would also help him win back some of the advertisers he had lost through the WOW-LASSIE campaign.

27: Class A

The judge appointed by the Lord Chancellor to hear the case against Mike Heron was Bertrand Bolster-Benedictine. But first, he was to hear evidence brought by the Maltese Government against Claudia Fortie for the murder of Laurence Tomas on Ramla Beach, Gozo. The two cases were held together because of the public protests organized by WOW-LASSIE, and the concerns of the police that their resources were being stretched to breaking point.

We join Bertrand Bolster-Benedictine on the way to the court as his car is barracked on both sides. One of the 'sex workers' had just offered him her Wednesday Morning Special whilst sitting on his bonnet, to which he screamed at his driver, Reggie, "Where the hell are the police?" and got the reply, "Doing their best sir. The crowds stretch for miles down the road."

"What the hell are yer blithering on about man? I've got to get into me courtroom. Else, I'll get a very a nasty missive from the Lord Chancellor."

Two girls from the 'pro group' were walking back to the Court from the public lavatory at Denham Groves Railway Station. One was dressed as a simple serving wench and the other a lady-of-class, with long skirts and a rather ostentatious floral hat.

"So," laughed the serving wench, "apparently in Victorian England a man was legally allowed to beat his wife, provided that he didn't use a cane thicker than his thumb."

"Which means," laughed the lady of class, "first thing to check before you got married was not the size of his cock but the thickness of his thumb."

Amidst the screams of laughter, the judge yelled to his driver, "If I am not in my courtroom within seven minutes, today will be the last in your seven years of service to me. In simple words, you'll be fired."

"*But sir*, look at these crowds."

"Run the buggers down, man."

"Now sir, *I think not,* but if you'd care to walk? Maybe slip your judges robe and wig on and you'll look like part of the protestors."

By this ploy, Bertrand Bolster-Benedictine was eventually ready to be seated in his judge's chair. The public gallery was crammed full, and he was waiting for the lawyers to take their places.

"I warn you Jenkins," he told his clerk, "if these girls in the public gallery start throwing their knickers at me, I shall clear the court."

"I did see in the Daily News," replied Jenkins, "that they claim each to be wearing ten pairs so security staff couldn't really stop 'em bringing 'em in."

"Let me know when to go in Jenkins. Hope this damn business is over by lunch. I fancy a trip to flights of -- umm, I mean -- my travel agent -- need to book my flights for --."

"Yes, sir. The Daily News claims that a woman has no culpability if a man dies during sexual excitement induced by her."

"Not sure if I agree with that, but he *was* a damn foreigner. Why the hell has all this landed in my "Because she is British, sir, and, as you know, Malta was ours until we made it independence. As part of the act of independence British courts still have sway, and this girl opted to be tried here."

"What the bloody hell is she up to giving some damn foreigner a blow job in his car on a beach?"

"Claims she was in mortal fear of her life --."

"And now I've got all these damn WOW-LASSIE women yelling and screaming. What the hell is going on, Jenkins?"

"Lord Chancellor thought you might as well deal with Claudia Fortie today and Mike Heron tomorrow, seeing as how WOW-LASSIE are making the headlines on both cases. In defence of Claudia, and prosecuting Mike."

Bertrand had been orphaned at age fifteen and was made a ward of court to his great uncle Sir Albert Bolster-Benedictine who had been chief land surveyor for the London District of Denham Groves. Willingly adopting the child, he changed his name, and sent him through the Law School at Oxford University and then had Mr Russell Doyle QC take him as a pupil. An endowment in Sir Albert's will to the Lord Chancellor's favourite charity, commonly known as 'the Lord Chancellor', ensured that when Albert passed away Bertrand become one of the youngest QC's ever appointed, and a month later he was a circuit judge. Sir Albert left the rest of his fortune to Bertrand, including his mansion in Denham Groves.

By contrast, Bertrand's sister was sent away by the court to a convent and never saw her brother again; he never enquired what happened to her. The nuns led her to believe that she could do anything with faith and the top of her wishes was to fly. She met the Bishop of Gostchester, who was Church of England Visitor to the

Convent when she was seventeen, and became his wife a year later to the great rejoicing of the nuns who were less than truthful with the Bishop as to the reason for their digging a deep moat around the convent that linked directly with the River Ozze.

In his younger days, Bertrand had earned a reputation as the playboy of London's West End and dated girls from every chorus line. It is rumoured that he sired many children, on whom he bestowed most of Sir Albert's fortune, private papers, and library.

The last time the judge had been called to London was for the trial of Denis Clerk who was accused of pushing his wife out the window of his office at the University of Oxenbridge. On seeing photographs of the woman he realised that she was the owner of the brothel and muttered, "Damn scoundrel this Clerk fellow. Now I've no one to give me a nice discount there. 'Flights of Fantasy' indeed. Turned out to be a prophetic name. Better give him a twenty stretch."

"Time to be seated, Judge."

There she stood in the court looking cool and calm and gave the judge a very wide-mouthed smile of the type that produced a deep craving in the judge's external tissues.

This was not a murder trial but a preliminary hearing to see if Claudia had a case to answer. The evidence was presented by the very suave Police Detective Dominic Fenech from Malta, dressed impeccably in a black suit, whiter-than-white shirt, with a dark-grey tie. Claudia was represented by an attorney, known in Britain as a barrister, from WOW-LASSIE named Sally Lyons-West. Kaye appeared as witness and related

Claudia's phone call to her from Gozo. The court was quiet as Claudia started to describe the scene on the beach but as she told of her head being forced into Laurie's lap and his sexual thrust to her mouth, the judge cleared the court and heard the evidence *in-camera*. Debauchery was a key feature of Bertrand's private life, but professionally, as a judge, he was an arch conservative and espoused the highest moral standards. After the court was cleared, Claudia, Kaye, Georgia, and PD Fenech approached the bench.

"I see no indication that Ms Claudia Fortie made any aggressive moves towards Mr Tomas," testified Fenech. "Quite the contrary, it would seem to me that he took advantage of her and there could even be a case for rape --."

"-- No, sir," interrupted Claudia. "He was very amorous, and I had no fear that he intended to hurt me. I enjoyed blowing him. Many girls do that to keep guys at bay. But I had no idea that he had some sort of weak heart --."

"Medical evidence," added PD Fenech, "shows that his genitalia where greatly enlarged and the car had been rocked so hard as to sink two feet into the sand."

Kaye's mouth was wide open in amazement and Sally looked at the judge and offered an opinion, "Sir, if I may ask permission to speak?"

"Yes, counsellor," replied the judge.

"Mr Tomas would appear to have engaged in sexual congress with my client of his own free will and therefore any ill effects to himself are entirely his own responsibility."

"I agree counsellor," responded the judge. "But there is one slight reservation. It is really a point of law."

"And that is *what*, sir?" she creased her face in genuine query.

"Did she do something to him that is outside the bounds of normal expectation? If I hire a painter to paint my house and he uses a method outside normal expectation and the house is damaged then he is at fault."

"Matter of interpretation, surely sir," she responded wanting to dismiss this case out-of-hand as due to male weakness.

Bertrand stared back at her determined to make the right decision.

"Suppose counsellor," he pondered, "that during sexual congress, a person deliberately hurts their lover. Is that murder or is that merely a risk taken in having sex with a person whom you cannot necessarily trust?"

Claudia responded with, "Sir, I have used that technique on men before."

"Is it something unique to you, Ms Fortie?" asked the judge.

There was silence as he looked at Claudia and then she replied, "I can describe it to you in private, sir."

"Let's adjourn for lunch," the judge replied and added, "I need extra evidence from you, Miss Fortie. Counsellor, I respect your need to be present, unless you wish to waive that right."

Sally sensed that her best chance of success in getting the case against Claudia dropped was to let her see the judge in private.

"I will waive that right, Judge."

200

As soon as the judge crossed the threshold between the court and his rooms he morphed back into Bertrand Bolster-Benedictine and sent his clerk Jenkins off to a long lunch.

So it came to pass that Claudia demonstrated her 'Class A' blowjob on Bertrand Bolster-Benedictine. When the court reassembled at 2 pm, the judge needed Jenkin's help to get to his seat and only just managed to pronounce that Claudia had no case to answer. Finding a 'Flights of Fantasy' business card in his wallet, he slipped it to Claudia after writing on its back, 'Suggest contact FF as you won't find other work til publicity over this case dies down'.

Kaye and Claudia went out that evening to celebrate, and in a highly-intoxicated state decided to visit Flights of Fantasy.

"Bloody good way to get our own back on these bloody men and make ourselves into rich women. Wonder how many we can kill in the first month," Claudia shrieked when told she could earn several thousand pounds a day with her class A technique.

The brothel owner had sat open-mouthed at, "Use my tongue, mouth and both thumbs as a clamp on the G spot."

In their taxi back to the station, Kaye had scolded, "Not only will you be damaged for life, but you are making money exploiting men which is just as bad as the exploitation of women."

"How is it exploitation when they pay *me*?"

"Well, then you are exploiting your own body to make money."

"Kaye, darling, that is nonsense. You only want to work for Mike Heron because you're bloody in love with him. How the hell do you imagine you'll change his Show? Anyway, I gather that BritishTV have cancelled it. So what sort of a job do you have with him now?"

28: Just a Puddle

Next morning Bertrand Bolster-Benedictine had some problems sitting as he waited to be called into his court in the case of WOW-LASSIE versus Mike Heron. Needing to pass urine, but afraid of the bad stinging felt last time, he was putting off that sensation for as long as possible. Also his genitals were expanded to such an extent as to put underwear at risk of mechanical failure.

"Sir," advised Jenkins, "maybe a quick visit to the toilet. Could be two hours before you can decently have the court rise once the case starts."

"Oh, I doubt it will take that long. I'm instructed by the Lord Chancellor to let him off with a caution. Gather that the Lord Chancellor himself likes the Mike Heron Show. Just a bit of fun and games on a Friday evening."

Thinking of 'a bit of fun and games on a Friday evening' had dislodged some of Bertrand Bolster-Benedictine's private parts, which were already delicate from his 'Class A', and he really needed to discretely rearrange himself as best he could.

"Jenkins, perhaps you're right. I had better have that leak before I go into court."

"Good idea, sir."

At that moment, the clerk of the court indicated to Jenkins that everything was ready and the judge could be seated in court as soon as he wished. Jenkins nodded and then, continuing to look at his newspaper, suddenly remembered the building work.

"Judge," he shouted at the judge's disappearing back, "the toilet facilities are temporarily moved to the other side of the main staircase."

Mr Justice Bertrand Bolster Benedictine heard the clerk distantly through the three layers of hanging plastic that he had pushed back en route to the place where the men's toilet had been since time immemorial. Many a judge had taken a well-earned piss there, whistling at the ceiling and thinking of his chances of promotion up the judicial scales. The old men's room had been painted green, as had most public lavatories in Britain prior to the arrival of the age of plastic.

"Damn clerk trying to tell me where the bloody lavatory is. Damn cheek."

Because of the importance of the Mike Heron Case, all workmen had been removed from the Court House for security reasons. So Bertrand Bolster-Benedictine walked ever onward constantly looking for the door of the lavatory and hoping that passing his water would not sting him.

"Here it is at last," he proclaimed to a particularly grimy piece of plastic sheeting and pushed hard on what he assumed was the lavatory door behind it. In reality he was pushing a piece of plywood that had been lightly tacked across a gap that was once a window. Still unsteady on his feet after his Class A, he experienced yet another new, and in a sense, equally liberating, feeling.

Out the window was a drop of about sixty feet and might just have been survivable had the construction company not also removed the pond. It was all part of a project to extend the Court House over which Denham

Groves District Council had agonized for months. There had indeed been some discussion as to whether the Mike Heron case could be heard before the building was closed for a year, but with the approaching end of the legal term, and because public interest and pressure were so great, it was agreed to hear the case but with the strict understanding that it could not extend beyond one week and that no other following case could then be heard. The hearing on the 'Gozo Murder', as Claudia's case was called by the popular press, had been slipped in before it at the last moment due to pressure from WOW-LASSIE; perhaps they believed it would build up momentum against the male chauvinist pigs.

As Bertrand Bolster Benedictine's own personal momentum increased vertically downwards, his body experienced what is called 'zero gravity'. It is exactly the same zero gravity under which astronauts work in space and is not due to a lack of gravity, as such, but rather a lack of ways to resist it. In zero gravity, Bertrand Bolster Benedictine's body changed shape: no longer a belly that hung flaccid, no longer genitals that hung limp and enlarged, no longer double chins that rolled down over his collar, no longer hair that fell uncut into eyes, reminding him of his need for a barber's appointment.

The judge's wig landed intact just a split second before his head. That may seem strange but is merely a consequence of all things falling at the same speed so that Bertrand Bolster Benedictine went down as a complete judge with wig on head, albeit that he was upside down. To be truthful there was a very slight, but perceivable, gap twixt wig and head due to air resistance from gowns aflapping. The wig seemed to lay waiting for the head to arrive at sixty miles an hour.

When a hard ball hits a floor, it bounces because it is almost perfectly elastic. As the ball softens it becomes less elastic until it lands plop on the ground and all its momentum is used to rip the ball apart.

Bertrand Bolster Benedictine's head proved to be remarkably elastic as it recoiled upwards, still attached to his shoulders and tunnelled vertically through his body.

The head made its vertical upwards exit between his legs.

Bertrand Bolster Benedictine trunk's continued downwards so that his skin turned inside out and a split second later there he stood on his feet as if skinned alive.

There was a momentary pause as the lines of his features and limbs started to blur and dissolve in the manner of a snow man on the first day of the spring thaw. The he collapsed like a massive dollop of red jam and ran outward to form a sticky, dark-red puddle. Onlooking birds and one dog arrived to sample Bertrand Bolster Benedictine before several small boys poked sticks into his remains.

The moral of this story for those intending defenestration is to take a good look below for small boys wandering aimlessly with sticks.

Paramedics arrived and, finding no body, decided to use buckets and mops to wash the last of Bertrand Bolster Benedictine away.

Just at that moment Police Sergeant Porkessen and Police Officer Knowles arrived with wailing sirens from the local police station.

"Here, stop that," yelled Police Sergeant Porkessen, "we need to draw a white chalk line around that puddle."

But it was too late. Bertrand Bolster Benedictine was flowing down a nearby drain, and so in a state of desperation the sergeant ran to the police car and grabbed an empty yogurt carton from his lunch box into which he scooped some of the last of the puddle. The tragic end of Bertrand Bolster Benedictine was complete when Mrs Jacqui Porkessen, emptying her husband's lunch box, poured the remnants of his 'Jacobs Fresh All Natural Yoghurt With The Fruit on Top' into the cat's dish and later commented, 'Well Puss, you certainly liked that, I must buy it again for you."

The Clerk of the Court announced that the Judge had left due to business with a higher authority. The case would therefore be postponed, upon which lawyers for BritishTV claimed that any new hearing would need to take place after the end of the legal term, and since the Mike Heron Show no longer existed, there would be no case to answer.

A white stretch limousine immediately left from the front of the Court with two attendant black Alfa Romeo cars riding shotgun, back and front. Mike asked Kaye about the battered, old, open-topped MG sports car trying to get up close to them.

"The driver's a woman," Kaye replied, "yes, I'm sure it's a woman. Very short. Sitting on a pile of cushions. No seat belt. Looks rather unsafe. She's got some sort of placard which she's holding up. Now she's standing on the cushions with it. What's it say? Okay, I can read it now. Yes, it's, *I'll get you for this, you bastard*."

"Nice turn of phrase," replied Mike. "A real credit to the British educational system."

At that point the road turned sharply right so as to cross over Hammersmith Bridge.

"Oh no, look Mike, she didn't make the turn. The car's gone down a boating ramp and she's sort of flying out the front window. She's in the air with her placard. Now, she's in the water. Okay, the placard makes a good float for her. No, no, she shouldn't try standing on it. Oh dear that must have been painful. It's alright, she's being rescued by a launch now. Nice looking boat. It's got a big advert on its side for the Mike Heron Show."

The judge's wig was left forgotten on the ground until Denny Groves picked it up a day later with tongs and sealed it in a plastic bag.

The legal profession likes to look after its own and the Lord Chancellor, who is the chief advocate in England, felt that Mike Heron had got off rather easily while Bertrand Bolster-Benedictine had a very rough deal. Going out the window of what was once the Judges 'Little Boys Room' was an unseemly end to a career, though totally lacklustre, was, nevertheless, one that deserved to be honoured in some way. Bertrand was after all a judge and, as Lord Chancellor, he couldn't allow frivolous lawsuits like WOW-LASSIE versus Mike Heron to lead to a judge going out the window to a gruesome demise.

There were pictures all over TV of the crowds outside the court and then the paramedics washing away the judge. Worst of all, Mike Heron had left triumphantly in that white stretch limousine with his extravagant show of wealth. Who the hell did he think he was? Damn kid from the suburbs. Arrogant Bastard. I think he needs a damn good twenty-stretch to cut him down to size.

Mike was arrested that evening and charged with man slaughter through contempt of court. The Lord Chancellor's clerk was told to schedule a woman judge to hear the case and picked the rather elderly Agatha Hornchurch QC who wrote to the Lord Chancellor from her home, Rosemary Cottage in Buckstead, and asked him what his bloody game was. After a phone call, she agreed to meet him at his club, 'The Boilermakers', in The Strand, and there they did a deal that she would hear the case in exchange for him writing to her neighbours, 'about their bloody dog, Henry, trying to hump her little white poodle, Janice, as soon as she stuck her little black nose outside the front gate of Rosemary Cottage'.

The knife was accordingly taken to Henry's nether regions and, with the taste of blood fresh in her mouth, Agatha sent Mike to the low-security jail at Hells Peak with the comment, "Teach you to respect women, Henry --, sorry I mean -- Heron. Why don't you have a year down there near St Fuller," and to herself, "damn fine job getting rid of that awful Bertrand Bolster Benedictine fellow. Tried to get into me pants at The Law Society Christmas Dance when I was a snippet of a girl, just on me first case."

Humpy attended the trial and as Mike was taken down slowly mouthed to him, "You're taking one for the team."

Mike smiled back in acknowledgement, knowing that he had never written a single line of the Shows and only appeared briefly at their beginnings and ends, where he dressed in an impeccable black suit and told two of his classic, harmless, Jack Benny jokes.

As a final gesture he mouthed back to Humpy, "Find Denny Groves for me."

29: The Mad Prof

It's time to check in one Denis Clerk. This chapter is not going to be very pleasant for us and so be warned but please try to work through it because it has much to say about us all. Okay, here goes.

Locking a human away for many years has one of two effects. Some men confined to a personal wilderness come out awash with ideas and resolutions which change the world; there are many examples from religion, politics and acadia. These men have egos and spiritualties that are bigger than any prison cell, and overcome the barren loneliness of a desert or the gross inhospitality of any mountaintop; they live within their own boundless imagination. Indeed isolation is a necessary condition for many works of great genius. Albert Einstein composed the greatest ever works of theoretical physics sitting alone, with a stack of writing paper and a pen. For such men, isolation fires deep cogitation which must not be broken by a single word from the outside world.

So let's go into the case of Einstein …. Whoops sorry wrong book. Okay, Denis Clerk.

Denis Clerk was not such a man of boundless vitality. Already broken, he could not survive alone. For Denis, the life-force had already gone.

When the Allied Armies liberated the Nazi concentration camp at Dachau, they found a population of humans who had become a sub-species. The doctors and nurses of the Allied liberators could not determine whether many of the bodies around the camp were alive or dead. All were dressed in long black and white striped shirts. Breathing was usually intermittent and low. An American nurse gave one of these men a small piece of chocolate which he immediately hid in a piece of toilet paper within his shirt. His intention was to wipe this piece of chocolate across his teeth each night and that would keep him alive. This is an act of unbelievable determination. It is the story of human survival over millions of years. But not all modern humans are capable of such spirit. Perhaps life imposes huge pressures on us so that 'survival of the fitness' leaves only the strong.

After the tabloids made the judgment that Denis had killed his wife and the murder was completely justified, they tended to drop the story, leaving Denis nothing more than an ordinary murderer. There were many more years to serve, and the days slowly merged into a continuum of meaningless drudgery.

Denis was always known in the prison as 'Mad Prof' or just 'Prof' for short. Two years after the tabloids had lost interest in him, Denis was asked for his real name by a fellow prisoner working in the kitchen, but Denis could not remember it.

Experts have shown that prison is hardest on intellectuals because they have such high expectations of their life in the world outside. An Australian researcher who was gaoled for murder of his wife escaped many times from a low-security prison and every time went to a nearby research institute to hear the latest developments in his field of science. And every year his case was reviewed by the prison board, and every time his plea for access to research journals was refused with the comment, "You are here to be *punished*." The next time he escaped, the prisoner went as usual to the research institute. Prison staff were alerted and arrived as usual expecting him to be chatting with the researchers. Instead they found him dead in the parking area: he had run up stairs to the top floor and gone out the window. In his pocket they found 365 sheets of toilet paper, saved at one a day over a year, on which he had scribbled in pencil a new scientific theory for the prediction of earthquakes.

Knowing what we love and hate is the basis of all punishment. It can be found in the techniques of parents who tell one child that there is no football until they have finished reading their library book and tell another child that there is no more reading until they have played football with their siblings. Denis's fellow inmates would enquire, "What d'you hate most in the world, Prof?" and in respond to Denis's answer, "Soccer," they would warn him, "Don't tell the screws that else they'll have you watching film of Manchester United, nonstop."

As we all get close to the end of life, or the end of our endurance, we tend to retreat into our childhood and demand the things of our childhood fantasies. We see old ladies with drawers full of baby toys and ancient millionaires with train sets.

Denis had a weekly ration of twenty cigarettes, and since he was a non-smoker, was able to trade it for special foods smuggled into the prison such as a tiny slice of his favourite New Zealand Cheddar Cheese made in the farms of the South Island. In this way, he opened himself up to compulsive shopping on the prison underground black market, known as 'Hells Peak Store'.

Towards the end of his fifth year of confinement, Denis had a visit from a prisoner known as Mott who was accompanied by two of his cronies. Prisoners tend to form gangs or tribes who protect one another against other gangs. The social system at Hells Peak was like that of the school yard at Denis's junior school: you needed to join a gang else you would be picked on endlessly. When he was six years old, a gang of boys had taken to following him around the yard and kicking him in the butt. One against six is unfair in any fight, and Denis had taken to standing with his back to the wall. The gang of boys then changed their tactics to frontal assault: they would try to knee him in the groin. His defence was simply to move along the wall but eventually they hit the spot and he doubled-over in pain. His cry for help brought an older boy named Jock Price and some of Jock's classmates to the rescue. Jock sized up the situation in a moment and picked up one of the tormentors in his two hands and held him high up against the wall, "If you ever attack this innocent little kid again, I'll tear your bleeding liver out and cook it for me tea, you little bastard," and to Denis, "Tell me if they try it again and we'll drag the little shits before the head teacher, who'll cane their arses, one by one.

Denis could see the social similarity between Hells Peak and the school exercise yard. In his eyes, Mott became Jock Price.

"Clerk, old boy," menaced Mott, "you are to organize a riot in the kitchen on Monday morning. I'll see you're well rewarded. Get you outside on a work detail in the main town in a month or two. Chance to see some skirt walking by, as you dig drains."

Denis, once a university professor, was reduced to a frightened animal.

"What time do you want the riot, Mott," Denis heard his own terrified voice reply.

"Start at eight thirty on the dot. Keep it going at least half an hour. I need all the screws in there dealing with the situation. Set up some fires. Fling oil on the gas burners and then cover it with wet towels and whatnot. Lots of smoke."

Isolation and loneliness does change the human character, and Denis went to work on the riot planning with gusto. His fellow kitchen workers were surprised, but the very mention of the name 'Mott' made them eager to help. Unfortunately, the riot and fire got out of hand and defeated its own purpose, which was to allow one of Mott's cronies to walk unnoticed out of the prison. With the arrival of almost every fire rescue vehicle within 10 miles, there was such a pack of incoming vehicles that not even a tiny mouse could have exited.

One of the benefits of the complete destruction of the kitchen was that the Army was called into the prison to set up a mobile canteen. This was the best food that the prisoners had ever eaten, and for his contribution, Denis achieved folk-hero status. But the new Governor, Eric Essenberg, had a different view of the situation.

"Clerk, you are a convicted murderer. You've openly admitted your guilt. The widespread antagonism against you, followed by the public sympathy that arose after you accused your late wife of being a witch, has already cost Robert King his job. I am now going to protect this prison, its inmates, and its staff against your further actions. Do you have anything further to say before you are sentenced to remedial punishment?"

"*Sir*," growled Denis with indignation, "I have been treated in the most abominable way and have had ignominy upon ignominy heaped upon me, based entirely on hearsay that I was responsible for some illicit intrigues at Oxenbridge University. What this prison has done is illegal and outside the authority vested in it by Her Majesty's Prison Service. I demand a full enquiry, retrial, and your removal from office."

Denis was put in solitary confinement for six months. The cell that measured ten feet by ten feet, he was totally alone for 183 days. Food and water were pushed through a tiny trap door, and he defecated and urinated into a hole in the floor.

When he was released back into his normal cell, he was a broken man. His head hung low, and unable to speak. After another three months, he was allowed to work in the new kitchens for two hours each week.

In the depths of mindless boredom, he would attempt to give an imaginary lecture on atmospheric circulation. Knowing that he must try for his own sanity and self-respect, he fixed an afternoon to stride back and forth across his cell pretending it was his first-year class. He could hear the noise from the students in his head but that was all. Why did air rise at the Equator? He had no idea.

So, it was hopeless. He might as well end it all. Using 'Hells Peak Store', he traded his next week's cigarette ration for a piece of rope. Now so thin, he could secrete the rope in the seat of his baggy pants. His supplier gave him advice. "I've given you six feet eight inches which is just enough. The knot is already tied. Now listen, this is what you do. Lasso the rope over the --."

But a warder had told them, "Get back to peeling them spuds, you two, else I'll have you peeling the bloody peelings."

Denis kept the rope hidden in his bed linen and then decided to leave the Earth during his 'personal time' on the afternoon of Easter Saturday. As soon as his cell door was shut, he got the rope in position and knew that he had an hour before the door was re-opened. On too many Saturdays he had sat staring into space until he could hear the warders starting to open cells at the far end of his corridor shouting, "Okay, you bloody wankers, time to put it away for another week." But this time they would open his door to see his feet swing back and forth in front of their eyes."

He sat on the edge of the top bunk hoping the knot was strong enough to kill him. Moving ever closer to the edge he could feel his bottom starting to slide. When he was a child, he would always slump forward in chairs and could hear his mother now, shouting out, "Denis, you will hurt yourself sliding forward like that. One day you'll break your neck. Please sit up straight," and he always did sit up, but this time was different.

If the knot broke, or failed to slide properly, he would crash to the concrete and be put in solitary confinement for another month. In the old days, prisoners were given two hundred lashes for attempted suicide and then three months buried up to their neck in the prison graveyard. The sadism of imprisonment dictates that the prisoners must be kept alive to endure ever more punishment.

Denis's bottom was sliding faster and he knew the end was near.

The cell door was opening as he swung forward, feeling the rope cut into his throat, burning away layers of skin and then that terrible throttling as his own weight tore the rope into his windpipe. The mechanical shock sent a pressure wave through his spine. His bowel was discharging just as if an enema had been pushed into him and he was urinating down his legs.

During most hangings, the hangee is paralyzed by pain before death and can only be revived if cut down within two seconds.

Denis's wrist watch ticked twice.

Two sets of prison warder's arms grabbed him and when he awoke next day in the prison sick room the rope was still attached to his neck with its end trailing on the floor. Still dressed in his soiled clothes, he was made to walk along all the prison corridors so that he could be seen by the other inmates. His walk of shame took him to Governor Essenberg's office.

"Clerk do you like heights?"

"No sir,"

"I tried so hard to reform you and make you into a decent citizen after you murdered your wife. I was in London last week for a lecture on the ultimate punishment for murderers. I'll try it on you. We'll take you to a spot that resembles the scene of your crime."

So they put Denis on the roof of Cell Block C which was a six-storey building. The rope was removed from his bleeding neck, but he received no other attention and only a jug of water each day, with a new ladle of prison porridge into his already mouldy spoon-less bowl. Defecating and urinating into his already stinking pants, he found nowhere to hang himself, and no rope, but on the edge of the roof, Governor Essenberg had ordered a wall built with an open window. It was the ultimate sadist punishment conceived by a sick mind.

The warders told him the door to the roof would be opened after a week and then he could come down if he was still alive.

"But Clerk, it's up to you to stay alert because we're commanded by the governor not to come up there and get you. Governor wants you to just sit and look at that open window."

Finally Denis was drawn to the window and would sleep with his head against it. Hating heights, he refused to look down and remembered as a child being too frightened to cross the shaky bridge that provided a shortcut home from school across the deep creek, and instead walked three miles to the main road.

Hidden deep in our psyches are personal fears and, as John Steinbeck tells us in his masterpiece, 'Nineteen Eighty Four', the art of the good tormentor is to find that fear. It may be snakes or spiders or big faces that appear at windows in the middle of the night, or perhaps the bird that is always hovering above us ready to dive. Some people have a need to touch any object with both hands. It's called obsessive compulsive disorder and they can be driven mad by a tormentor who refuses to allow them the second touch.

Denis's great fear was height. This was really the reason he had not reported his wife's fall out the window. To him it was unbearable to think of anything falling. To prevent himself from doing so, he formed a deliberate mental block.

Forming a mental block is quite easy and something many people do occasionally: perhaps they owe taxes and so refuse to open mail from the tax authorities. Maybe they refuse to call their doctor to get results of blood tests that they think could show they have a fatal disease.

Perhaps if Denis had overcome his fear of looking down, he would have felt such a relief that he could have gone out the window. It would have been equivalent to a man with a phobia about owing taxes, who drinks himself stupid, gets in a rage and yells at that letter from the tax authorities; he rips it open only to find a huge refund.

"I will do it," Denis repeated to himself endlessly all day and night. His eyes got ever closer to the edge and his love-hate obsession with the window got ever greater as his heart pumped and the adrenaline caused his mind to lose focus, with urine pouring warm down his legs in the one great pleasure left to him. Finally, his eyes were just at the edge and he dumped faeces into his pants with an explosion of gas that felt like the wind of the angels blowing him to eternity: no more prison,

"Yes," he yelled. "Sod them all. Here I come --."

Big arms went around him and a gentle voice, "I'm your new cell mate. Let's get you down and back on the bunk.

Denis woke a day later in the medical wing of the prison with a multitude of tubes into his nose, mouth and arm. There was a face watching him that he recognized from a TV Show. It had a big smile and whispered softly, "I'm your new cell-mate. Rest now, Denis, don't try and talk. Just rest. We're going to get you well again. By the way, I'm Mike Heron, the comedian."

30: Going to St Fuller

Let us recall the very first governor of the prison, Robert King, telling Denis that he could go out for days and enjoy the local countryside whilst he was waiting for his appeal to be heard. It was all a lie of course and the governor was just trying to get some personal kudos in the newspapers by seeming to be such an understanding and broad minded person.

The governor painted in our minds a very informal gaol which had a charming old rustic front gate through which Denis could walk with the merest wave of his day pass. I certainly imagined Denis stopping at a quaint little pub, a hundred yards down the road and enjoying a quiet pint chatting to the locals with maybe a few warders on their way to work passing on a few jokes about the clownish behaviour yesterday of inmates in block A. Then Denis would saunter down to St Fuller and enjoy the comings and goings on the quay, watching the fishing boats unloading their bounty, before being tempted to a fresh crab sandwich at the 'Fruits of the Ocean' café washed down with a glass of Guinness; which I should recommend to you reader as the ideal lunch in St Fuller. Then a very leisurely stroll back to the prison where the guard greeted him with, "Good night, sir. Hope you had a good day. By the by, I've left a pot of your favourite orange marmalade in your room made by me daughter. Took the opportunity to give you fresh sheets and change your towels." Listening to the old rustic gate close with that characteristic squeak, Denis realised that he was as happy as at any time in his life. Going straight to bed, he pulled up the sweet smelling sheets around his neck and dreamt of the new lambs skipping down the lush green hillside when he was a boy in New Zealand.

Now reader, I have to disillusion about everything that Robert King told us.

The sad truth is that there is a security zone around the prison and only vehicles with special passes are allowed within ten miles.

A special bus leaves St Fuller at 10 am on Wednesdays and Fridays, then stays at Hells Peak for two hours. Passengers must have a permit from the prison Governor and three forms of picture identity. Entry to the bus requires a body search by a prison guard and scrutiny of all bags. This search is repeated at the prison and passengers then wait in an anteroom until called into the main visiting room where they are seated at tables. 15 minutes later their assigned prisoner comes and sits opposite at the same table, but no physical contact is allowed, and for ten minutes there is no talking. Five prison warders patrol the room and signal when talking may commence. At no time may visitors or prisoners place their hands or any object on, or below, the table between them.

Would-be-visitors are screened by the Governor, who judges their suitability. It is rare for a prisoner to be allowed more than one visitor at a time, unless they are immediate family.

But, fortunately for us, Mike Heron was not so much a prisoner as a jail hero. These were not the days, or the prison, where prisoners could watch TV, but Mike's reputation had spread across the western world, and to have him at Hells Peak was to change the prison from a dark, evil hole to a place filled with gentle comedy.

It was as if a light had suddenly been turned on and the inmates felt bright and happy. If the Disney Organisation ever decide to make a movie of our story there will surely put little laughing chipmunks swinging from every cell door and fawns skipping as light as feathers along the corridors.

But above all else, the prisoners wanted the Mike Heron Show, with all the girls and the slapstick. Prisoners who had been at Hells Peak for many years, and would be there for many more, suddenly felt the breath of hope.

The yearning.

The deep yearning for life.

The yearning for youth and beauty.

The yearning for escape from captivity of body and mind.

Mike Heron had done nothing but bring pleasure to millions. And to men that was the pleasure of their manhood. The worst thing that interment does to a human is to take away a prisoner's purpose on Earth, and for men that is to take away their manhood. Mike Heron taught us all to laugh and to enjoy farce.

Suddenly the warders and prisoners were friends as they exchanged Mike's quips such as, "The best way of keeping us in here would be a bar inside rather than bars on windows". That one went round all blocks in minutes followed by, "There is to be a new law that convicted men must take their wives with them to prison. Being locked in a cell with your wife for twenty years should cure all serious crime."

Some of Mikes jokes were tailored to the harsh reality of prison life including what he called his 'limited circulation humour' in which he responded to 'Gay' Gordon's request for a 'bit of dirt' with, "There is so much homosexuality in this prison that I realise why they talk about 'being sent down for twenty years.'

Susan Yates had been appointed to replace Governor Eric Essenberg three days after Mike arrived. This followed an illicit telephone call by Mott, the prison bully, to the News of Britain allowing Mike to describe the treatment of Professor Denis Clerk on the roof of Cell Block C, including a photograph of the fake window. The headline was 'Sadist Prison Governor tells inmate to go 'Out the Window'.

Part of the new breed of prison staff, Susan believed that the purpose of prison is to reform criminals. She also had an 'open office door' policy in which any prisoner could book an interview with two days notice. Mike was the first to avail himself of this privilege and told Susan of his idea to bring his show to Hells Peak.

"Good idea, Mike. I love that show. Really funny. But, one condition. All of the organization must be done by prisoners. And also, there must a fair number of sketches with some sort of intellectual content. I saw you when I was a student at Oxenbridge doing skits based on Shakespeare. Look Mike, I am never going to get this pass the Head of the Prison Service, Sam Wheatcroft, unless there is a major educational element to the Show. How about having somebody give the Shakespearean background?"

"Ma'am, I know the perfect person for the job. Name's Denny Groves. A research student of Judith

Cooper at Royal Sunbury. I'll write him a letter if that is allowed."

"Please be discrete, Mike. Please. Please. Else I'll get the boot from this post and I can only do good while I actually have this job."

As Mike walked into the visitor's room on his first Wednesday at Hells Peak, he was breaking many rules with the connivance of the new Governor.

The first was that he should not have been allowed visitors for one month. The second was that he knew his visitor was lying about her sex; Humpy wore heavy clothes and a cloth cap. Third, Humpy gave Mike a book while the warders turned their heads. It was the script of the first Mike Heron Show ever to be performed outside the BritishTV Studios. It also contained the address of Denny Groves and a note from Kaye Fortie.

The next Wednesday, when Mike again walked into the visitors' room, he met Denny Groves.

"So Denny, Audrey Smith wrote to BritishTV a month ago saying that you had gone missing and since I am your cousin, she thought I might know your whereabouts."

"Shush. Lower your voices, you two."

"Mike, I discovered the truth about the River Telmer after falling from a balcony through a hole in the railings and landing in a deep pond."

"How deep?"

"Ten or twenty feet. Quite narrow. I sort of slide against the sides and was then washed along an underground culvert and bloody scared out of my mind. I was full of wine and vomited like hell. In fact, I felt that this must be hell. You know all dark and slimy."

"You could have drowned?"

Most other voices had lowered so as to listen to Mike who was everybody's hero.

"To be honest," answered Denny, "there was not that much water and after a few minutes I climbed ashore in an underground cave where the river formed a huge subterranean lake with limestone outcrops, walls, stalactites and stalagmites. The amazing thing about it was the heat. The water was steaming as if I was in a tropical jungle."

"I hear that some of these buried rivers are heated geologically. You know, from the Earth's natural inner heat. Saw a program on TV."

"That must be it, Mike. I suddenly felt bloody fish trying to eat my toes and discovered that the bottom of the lake was black with what I later discovered were Piranha fish."

"Heck."

"There was a set of rough steps up. I felt like some character in one of those comic books we read when we were kids. You remember?"

"Oh yes. I loved 'em. And listening on the radio to 'Dick Barton, Special Agent' pursued by the forces of evil."

The room was now dead quiet. These were men of a generation that remembered the famous Dick Barton nightly series on BBC radio. Eyes glanced over as prisons and warders thought back to those halcyon days.

"So, Mike, did you know those Piranha fish can jump?"

"Now, Denny, you're suffering from hallucinations."

"Not a bit of it. I've done a lot of research on this, and there is a fellow at the London School of Tropical

Aquatic Science that claims that Piranha will adapt quickly to find food."

"How does jumping get them food in the sterile cave?"

"So here is the second of my revelations. Atop the banks of the river are dozens of cats."

"Domestic cats?"

"My theory is that these cats have been washed down the river from homes upstream."

"Perhaps they fell down that same pond as you did."

"Could be. Well, my theory is that the cats arrived in the cave and started trying to catch the fish. You know the way cats will try to fish by waving paws in the water. Just the same way that they go for the goldfish in the aquarium in your living room. So the fish hit back at them by jumping and it's now a sort of dynamic balance."

"That's quite a story. So you got out of the water and pushed your way past the cats, Denny?"

Warders looked at watches but it was clear that nobody wanted to move.

"Yes, I climbed out with a few Piranha fish hanging to my pants and there I was in the grounds of a magnificent house that I later discovered was owned by Bertrand Bolster-Benedictine, who, as you know, was my father. I was greeted in the yard by hordes of dogs and yet more cats."

"Hordes of dogs? You mean domestic animals?"

"Basically yes, but obviously running wild."

"Feral dogs can be pretty vicious, Denny."

"Well these were all very placid and overfed. I later discovered that Bertrand Bolster-Benedictine was feeding them. There was a whole family of German Dachshunds."

The name Bertrand Bolster-Benedictine was greeted with dismay by some of the prisoners but all of them, and their visitors, were much too enthralled with the conversation to move.

"But Bertrand was away so much, that he must have had some staff to help him."

"He did. Fellow called Alex. Apparently Alex arrived on Bertrand's doorstep one Friday evening via the same route as me except he'd been walking his dog Fritz. Claiming the status of a marital refugee, Alex couldn't go home to his wife without his dachshund, Fritz, and dear Fritz was not willing to leave what he considered the garden of paradise where he could roam free."

"Sounds like Fritz set up his own tribe in that garden when he arrived with Alex. It's really a wonderful story of liberation. Fall into a pond and end up in a magic garden. Almost like a Victorian children's novel."

"Well Mike it's not quite as simple as that. You only end up in the cave if you climb out of the river. Else you're eaten alive, although some heavy inedible objects are carried down river into the Thames."

"So Denny, you came out of the cave into the garden of a house. What's the house called?"

"Called 'Sunken Rivers' and was apparently built by Sir Albert Bolster-Benedictine who was surveyor for the Denham Groves district. I guess that was where I was conceived, which is why Mum called me Denham, or Denny, Groves."

Gasps of astonishment from the women.

"So you went home and dried off, Denny?"

228

"That I did, Mike. Spent the next few months researching that river and also my father. Turns out he had a sister who was the mother of that woman Sylvia Clerk, who was murdered by her husband, or supposed to have been murdered by him, you know, the geographer, Denis Clerk."

"You mean that Sylvia Clerk was the niece of Bertrand Bolster-Benedictine who tried the case against Denis? Bloody hell that invalidates the trial."

All eyes on Mike.

"And while we're talking about that case, I found an old metal brief case at the side of the lake. Rusted as hell it was, but I took it home and slowly cleaned it up and got it open. It's basically an autobiography by this Sylvia Clerk woman. I think that Denis should publish it. Certainly removes any guilt from him and should be a best seller with all that corruption and murder, plus her crazy, bloody mother going flying 'out the window'."

There was not a sound from the room and, although visiting time was well past, the warders stood with their mouths open wide.

"Anyway Mike, you said you had a favour to ask me. Incidentally, I found all of Sir Albert's maps of the drains in Denham Groves marking the course of the River Telmer all the way down to Cayho-on-Thames. There is talk in Telmer St Joseph, you know, the place where Denis and Sylvia lived, that all sorts of precious stuff has been smuggled down the Telmer to the Thames in the past."

The Bishop, Comedians, ...

31: Clowns and Eels

Denis was released next day, and moved into Mike's home, where he was reunited with Rustler, who now only answered to the name 'Rusty'. Organizing movement of the Teddington staff to Hells Peak Prison was now simple, and he spent the rest of his time working on Sylvia's book. The British government gave him a full reprieve and a large cash payment for wrongful imprisonment. News of Sylvia's book was leaked to the press by warders from Hells Peak, and most then resigned and opened pubs with names like, 'The Mad Prof', 'Out The Window', or 'Mrs Clerk'.

The Mike Heron Show never made it to Hells Peak, because with remission for good behaviour, Mike was released after serving only 5 months of his sentence. The day before his release he wrote to Audrey Smith, and his letter reached her just as she finished packing to return to Australia; Judith had been made Vice Chancellor of the new University of Rottnest in Western Australia, which was heavily endowed by Cooper Graceman International Foods.

Publicity from Sylvia's book so frightened the owner of the Flights of Fantasy brothel that she offered it for sale. It was bought by Claudia and its name discretely changed to 'The Class A'.

Mike married Humpy, and they are living at Sunningham where they have founded the now famous Mike Heron Comedy Studios onboard 'Wandering Cloud', which is parked alongside their dock. The studios are run by Humpy, with all the female staff from Teddington prancing the decks in their alluring gear.

Tim Paul finally admitted defeat in trying to live in Caithness and took the train south and arrived with a lot of luggage at Sunningham and rang the bell. Hearing a voice below her, "Humps, I really need to get back to clowning. It's part of my basic character. I'm stymied as a person unless I make people laugh," Humpy looked down and screamed in delight, "It's my favourite clown, *Tiny Tim*."

"Humpo darling, I need to get back on tour and make people laugh in the towns and villages."

"Mike is the same way, Tiny. Why don't you two do a stand-up comedy world tour of Britain? I can't go. I'm pleased to announce that Mike and I have our own little star in production."

So Mike and Tiny Tim joined forces and toured as the comedy act: 'Look B4U Leap'.

Sophia Fletcher came home early one afternoon and found a pair of female legs protruding 12 inches over the end of the short Fletcher marital bed. There are times when we should all know where we can immediately put our hands on a tube of superglue. Waking with one's feet glued together is a situation which causes stress and is very difficult to explain away to one's husband over that evening's dinner.

Grabbing her two kids, Sophia moved to Saunders Bonk in Somerset, Southwest England, where she got a job in an orchard picking apples. A year later 'Look B4U Leap' was performing at the Coliseum Theatre, City of Bath, and so she found a sitter and had a night out.

"Nothing changes," she screamed halfway through the show. "Look, bloody goose bumps." After the Show she found her way back stage intending to assail Mike, but was intercepted by a very pregnant Humpy who had driven down to Bath to see her husband.

"Sorry, Miss. Mike's not available at the moment, but let me introduce you to Tiny Tim. He's just off for a drink, and I'm sure he'd love some company." So it came to pass that Sophia Fletcher became Sophia Paul and Tiny Tim had an instant family with two sons.

Kaye Fortie married Denny, and they went to live in 'Sunken Rivers', Bertrand Bolster-Benedictine's house in Denham Groves. Police Sergeant Porkessen managed to rescue a tiny drop of Bertrand Bolster-Benedictine that had been missed by the cat and they buried him in the rose garden of 'Sunken Rivers'.

Kaye and Denny had three sets of twins: Michael and Denis, Claudia and Skye, Joanie and Josephine. This proved that Kaye's mother's ranting about her daughter's pre-menopausal conditions was, to use a technical term, a lot of maternal hogwash.

The River Telmer still flows during wet summers and spreads out in a brown plume across the Thames at Cayho. Denny still hunts for river debris in the subterranean lake beneath 'Sunken Rivers', and the children have made it their own secret world.

For those who wish to visit 8 Pemberton Road, the house is still there, but it is important to say that Ralph Rankworth-Humphries's pond was unfortunately filled in when the road was widened. On the good side, there have been no further missing dogs or cats.

The postman who was missing with the annual tax notices for Denham Groves, and whom we might have suspected of falling down the pond, was in fact living comfortably in Worthing, Sussex enjoying the fruits of a very large sum of gold coins which he found washed onto the small front lawn of 8 Pemberton Road. They were the last of the loot fenced to Patrick Larkin a century before and finally washed from their hiding place in Telmer St Joseph by a gigantic storm.

Frank Kent and his wife Bunny sold their now defunct TV Company and bought the eeling business from their old friend, Joanie, who had finally decided to retire. Frank sold the eels worldwide - frozen, canned and boil-in-the bag under the name, 'Sweet Kent Eels', and Bunny settled down to write a book about Mike and Hump, and their comedy show, called, 'What a Pair'.

If life is ever dull, go and watch some comedians; they are always there for you. But please be careful of high windows.

Unfortunately, we must finally relate that Frank Kent, died unhappily. Let us admit that while we are truly sorry, we did have a certain resentment against him for his wanting to take money from Humpy when he closed down the show. Also there was evidence that it was he that exploited the original sexual innuendos in the Show to drive up the audience figures and make money.

So, the sad story is that while entertaining buyers aboard *Wandering Cloud* one evening, Frank had the need for a toilet and made the same mistake as had Sophia with the sign *WC: h*e splashed into a strong flood tide on the Thames at Cayho. His stomach being heavy with Kentish Eel Pie, he sank immediately and ended up at the subterranean entry to the River Telmer which had always been a prime spot for catching eels; the following year they were fatter than ever.

Otherwise, like all good fairy stories, they all lived happily ever after. Just in closing, we should say the Oliver brothers, and their wives, after making a world famous success of the Theatrical School of Wendsor County, retired and bought almost identical cottages with orchards in Saunders Bonk in Somerset.

Oh, sorry there is one tiny thing that came to light just a year of two after our story had concluded. Denny became a real expert on the buried River Telmer. Interested in the river after it passed 'Sunken Gardens', his home with wife Kaye, he wanted to map its route into the Thames. With a motor, search lights and batteries, he slowly made his way downstream. There were plenty of ventilation shafts so the journey was not as terrifying as we might suspect. Then one evening his head crashed into the feet of a skeleton hanging vertically from a tree root which had penetrated its way into the sunken river.

The explanation was indeed very simple. When she fell into the pond, the Duchess of Wessex had apparently been drowned and swept downstream at full flood to be subsequently impaled on the tree root where her remains found their way into 'Smithers Bitter Sweet Eel.' That's why Smithers claimed it tasted like her. You thought *what*? Really. Smithers did what?

When Humpy realised that the skeleton was her grandmother, it was buried alongside her late husband.

The End

PS: Details of Claudia's 'Class A' technique can be found in her book 'Thumbs Up, Girls'.

Cast

Agatha Hornchurch (Judge)

Albert Bolster-Benedictine (Surveyor)

Alowishus Bates (Duchess Wessex's cousin)

Andrew Mathias (Head of Geography prior to Denis)

Anglican Bishop of Gostchester

Audrey Smith (student from Australia)

Aunty Nelly (Doris's sister)

Barbara (Bunny) Warren (Frank's wife and journalist)

Bertrand Bolster-Benedictine QC (judge)

Bill Wolfson (secretary, Committee on Climate)

Brian Jackson (head of technical section)

Carole Bates (Billie's, whoops, sorry, George's wife)

Celia Bolger

Claudia Fortie

Denham (Denny) Groves (Mike's Cousin)

Denis Clerk (the professor)

Dirk (or Derek) Young (university assistant registrar)

Duchess of Wessex

Elizabeth Rankworth-Humphries (present Duchess Wessex)

Frank Kent (owner of BritishTV)

Geoffrey Tate (Head, Aeronautical Engineering)

George Bates (Alowishus's son)

Guy Holmes (Sylvia's friend)

Hon Pamela Horsham-Goodwin (Mark's cousin)

Humpy the Clown

Iris Bunsbury (the late Duchess of Wessex)

Joanie Rankworth-Humphries (daughter, Lady Wessex)

Joe Oliver (Mr Oliver's brother)

Johnnie Walker (seaman)

Laurie Tomas (Gozzo car rental)

Kaye Fortie

Magdalena (Bishop's wife)

Mark (owner, Sloane Street Investment Bank)

Michael (Mike) Heron

Mr Lauder (Mike's mathematics teacher)

Mr Oliver (Mike's teacher)

Omegustus Bunsbury (the late Duke of Wessex)

Patrick Larkin (Sam's father)

Paulo (Claudia's waiter)

Percy Warrington (George Bates friend)

Peter Erho (International Mining Systems)

PD Dominic Fenech (from Gozo)

PO Porkessen and PO Knowles

Ralph Rankworth-Humphries

Robert King (first warden of Prison)

Roger Stringer (retired geographer)

Roselyn and Alex Harbury (parents of Fritz)

Roy Bolger (staff member of Geography)

Ryan Jones (Claudia's husband)

Sally Lyons-West (WOW-LASSIE lawyer)

Sam Larkin (real name of Smithers)

Skye (Mike's friend at College)

Smithers (Butler)

Sophia Fletcher (Mike's antagonist)

Susan Yates (Prison Governor)

Sylvia Clerk (Denis's wife)

Tim (Tiny) Paul (Clown)

Tony Fletcher (Sophia's first husband)

Veronica Warrington (or was it 'Valery', Percy's wife)

Wally and Doris Heron (Mike's parents)

PSS: That's it. I hope you also enjoy my other books which are listed below. While you read them I might try flying out the window. Here I go. Wow it is quite fun. Thud, I'm on the ground already.

Let me find a higher window. This will do: it's on the fourth floor. Blast that's locked. Up one more flight. Yes, this should do it. Here we go.

Oh what a feeling. I'm weightless. Some damn bird just dropped a message on me. Oh bother, the ground is coming up rather fast.

Please don't try this at home. Okay, let's stop kidding. This is only a book. So, I have air brakes and can stop and then go back and so have you. See you soon.

Clifford J. Hearn
March 2015

The Bishop, Comedians, ...

Other books by Clifford J. Hearn

The Hepsom Abbey Saga

Book 1: Star Crossed Lovers

Book 2: Hepsom Abbey

Book 3: Cassie's Quest

Book 4: The Fall

Book 5: Falling Like Snow

Book 6: Inheritance

Book 7: Rape and Murder

Book 8: Lord Hepsom

Peter and Joe Trevelyan Stories

1. The Seymour Affair
2. The St Ives Affair
3. The Holy Murders

Short Stories

1. Pious Diner
2. Drone Wars: Europagnis 2030
3. George Seagull
4. The Notes
5. Watching Boy

Other Books

1. Brunel University: Early Days
2. The Science Industry
3. Dynamics of Coastal Models

43425230R10137

Made in the USA
Charleston, SC
24 June 2015